STREAMING NOW

STREAMING NOW

LAURIE STONE

POSTCARDS FROM
THE THING THAT IS HAPPENING

dottir
press
NEW YORK CITY

Published in 2022
by Dottir Press
33 Fifth Avenue
New York, NY 10003
dottirpress.com

Parts of this book have previously appeared in some fashion in the *Women's
Review of Books, Evergreen Review, n+1,* and *Taint, Taint, Taint*.

First printing 2022

Text design by Frances Ross
Cover design by Andrew Saulters

Trade Distribution through Consortium Book Sales and Distribution,
www.cbsd.com.

Library of Congress Control Number: 2021948459
ISBN 978-1-948340-52-6
eBook ISBN 978-1-948340-53-3

MANUFACTURED IN THE U.S. BY MCNAUGHTON & GUNN Inc.

Dottir Press takes a feminist approach to publishing and artistic production,
working to fill the absences in both our history and present culture through
storytelling in all forms and for all ages.

For Richard Toon

And for the women's movement

Contents

Part 1: Pandemica, Hudson, New York

Part 2: Elsewhere, Elsewhen

Denouement: New York City

When my sister was dying, I would walk in the city morn-ings and sit on a bench and write what came to mind, and I got to thinking of these exercises as "postcards." I was writing to her from a specific place and also writing to everyone from anywhere. What makes both true is the intimacy of the writer's voice—my voice—and an atmo-sphere of missing connection to others and wishing to show them where you have landed.

I have been writing in this form since then. What is the form? You could see it as a series of "meanwhiles." Also, as a series of "yes, ands"—the prompt that spurs improv—instead of "no, buts." I have been wondering how to describe what people will read in this book, composed almost entirely of these intimate dispatches that, gathered together, form an atmosphere. I have been thinking about what that atmosphere is and hoping it offers readers some-thing of the pleasure of opening another person's diary, or finding a photo album in a flea market that so concretely conjures an elsewhere and an elsewhen, you can enter it.

In a journal entry, Susan Sontag wrote, "One of the main (social) functions of a journal or diary is precisely to be read furtively by other people, the people (like parents + lovers) about whom one has been cruelly honest only in the journal."

That is one approach, and I think this book invites something of the overheard of life and the caught-in-the-act of life, the dashed-off idea that can be exaggerated and raw. In my case, especially in my slash-and-burn takes on events and images I understand as woman hate.

The mood of this book is more loving than angry—more loving than anything else, as I read through it. A friend recently said of life, quoting a family refrain, "We're all just walking each other home." The words touched me, and I thought they were true, and when I can understand life this way, it makes me miss everyone I have ever loved, including people who let go of me because they could not go on as we had.

I love talking to you and making you laugh. I don't believe in private writing, really. I think it can hurt the way you write a sentence.

PART 1

Pandemica
Hudson, New York

HUDSON, New York, March 28, 2020

I bought a forsythia bush in a farm store and was scared all the time. I bought purple pansies for when the frost ends.

Psychoanalysis says you can stop a thing by understanding its origin. The brains of *homo sapiens* will make up a story with any random things laid out in a row. The brains of *homo sapiens* will find a plot. That is the brilliance of the jump cut in film. We think we can see where something is going from where it has been, and we think we know where a thing came from because of the way it turned out. We can't do either of these things.

I asked the man I live with if, to exist, virtue needed a lack of virtue in the picture for comparison. He said, "No." I said, "The concept of virtue feels Christian to me, and I don't like it." He said, "It started with the Greeks." I said, "I feel vulnerable." I said, "Saying 'I feel vulnerable' adds a layer of vulnerability."

A friend emails to say he is jealous I still have Lysol when it's off the shelves in New York. Another friend emails to say, "I don't want to see pictures of your rocks. I want to move my own rocks." It's risky to be happy.

Last fall the man I live with and I bought a house no one else wanted in upstate New York. It wasn't finished. The trees were tangled up in hairy vines of poison ivy. The former owners were hoarders and used their woods as a dump. The man I live with is a type 1 diabetic. In the event of infection by COVID-19, his chance for pneumonia is ten times higher than the rate for other people. Years ago, when a man I was with was dying of bone marrow cancer, he kept wanting to live, and some people—I could tell from their faces—saw this as a form of gluttony.

The other night I had my first virus dream. I wander into the opening of an art gallery, where there is fancy food and trays of drinks. People urge me to taste everything, and I shovel in hors d'oeuvres as a voice in my head says, "Wash your hands! Get the hell out of there! People are too close!" But the food is free.

We are clearing the woods on our property. We are raking leaves and cutting down sick trees and hauling things to the dump, readying the land for planting. We are watching mysterious green spikes poke up. The other night I noticed a small blister on my wrist. It itched. More blisters rose up. Every time I looked at my body there were more ribbons of blisters. It was like Linda Blair in *The Exorcist*, lashed by the devil.

Type 1 diabetes is an autoimmune disease caused when a genetic predisposition meets an environmental trigger. The beta cells in the pancreas stop producing insulin. The man I live with was twenty-three when he was diagnosed, and at that time his life expectancy was many years shorter than the amount he has lived so far. He was told he would likely lose a limb or two and go blind. There were no continuous glucose-monitoring pumps. He had to inject himself with glass hypodermics that had thick needles he would boil in a pan. He had to adjust to the disease or die slowly of organ damage or die quickly of high or low sugars. As new technologies became available, he learned to insert catheters into his body, as well as, in time, a subcutaneous sensor. There is no cure for his disease. There are no treatments, really, other than the tight control of blood sugars. He is less anxious than I am about contracting COVID-19. He has already lived most of his life inside disease.

Books and films that take place before the pandemic seem to be missing a leg or a head, limping along, innocent of what they could not know. The man I live with says, "I want to plant things my father grew in his garden. Did you know rhubarb makes a groaning sound as it grows?" I say, "Let's go to Agway," and we put on our gloves and masks and drive there. We look at shovels. The only one the right size feels too heavy. There are boxes of rhubarb kits. I'm not sure what's inside them. As I approached the counter, a man says to the woman at the register, "Yeah, the bars are open. The problem is the old people, making a big deal for everyone else." I put down the rhubarb box and say to the man I live with, "Let's get out of here."

We have been watching season two of *My Brilliant Friend*, based on the novels of Elena Ferrante. The story, set in Naples and beginning in the 1950s, studies two women who are allies and competitors and whose intimacy is again and again interrupted by men. Men who, without consequences, beat the women in their lives, sell them into disastrous marriages, threaten murder and make good on it. It's dull. True and relentless and dull. I love looking at the faces of the two young women who play Lila and Lenu, so young and oddly hushed in their delivery. Even speaking to each other alone, they have fashioned a kind of code speech that says: *Everything I say to get by in the world is a lie.*

I said to the man I live with, "After the age of the virus becomes the age of what that next age will be called, one thing will remain." He said, "What?" I said, "The hatred of women for being women." He said, "It's good to have something to believe in."

The other day I offered free books to anyone who wanted them. I put two boxes at the end of the driveway with a sign that asked people to wear gloves and take what they wanted. People came by. We spoke at a distance. One box of books was gone. A woman brought her kids, who stayed in the car. It was the first time they'd been out for a while.

When my sister was dying, the room I was sleeping in was hot, and l would slip down to the living room, where the air conditioning was better, and where, from the couch, I could see the piano that had sat in the home of our parents. I think all the time of calling my sister. A few days before she died, she put glaucoma drops in her eyes, saying, "In case I wake up tomorrow and don't have cancer anymore."

I said to the man I live with, "We need to have living wills and medical power of attorney." He said, "Why, is someone going to die?"

A friend writes to say she is looking forward to walking in the city again. A place without streets you cannot walk on for miles is not a city. Another friend is planning to leave the place where she is sheltering in two or three months. People want to believe in an After from which they will be able to grasp the thing they cannot see from the Now. As *Game of Thrones* moved toward its conclusion, I lost interest. No one cares about the ending of anything.

HUDSON, New York, April 2020

Three things in the moment you love? I'll start.

The flat, gray sky that is almost the same color as the snow-covered fields. The Chopin impromptu on the radio. A plaster parrot with a green back and yellow breast that is swinging on a tree outside the window. I love this parrot.

Some months ago I was asked to describe a book I'd written in a sentence of any length. I didn't write the sentence. I thought for a while the reason I didn't write the sentence was the election and the pandemic. I don't know the reason I didn't write the sentence. Instead, I've been thinking about writing I want to read. The sentences I want to read are little provocations that mount up like a road accident.

And something else: if I am your reader, and you are reporting a scene of violently ordinary sexism—say, the way males in a particular culture get to walk ahead and females by custom and possibly by law are required to jump over a cliff onto jagged rocks, a different woman every few minutes—and the thing you are talking to me about is the conversation the men are having as they stroll ahead, deaf to the cries of the women on the cliffs, if you report this conversation, full of meaning to the men and to you, if you report this conversation without telling me as well how the rest of the scene is making you feel and what it is making you think about, if you do this, I will cease to be your reader.

This is not an example of cancel culture. The reader needs to fall in love with what the narrator is in love with, and how can you be in love with what the narrator is in love with if the narrator is in love with a world bent on your destruction? Cancel culture is when you arrive at this point and then insist no one else should read what you don't want to read.

I streamed four shows over the past few weeks, all centering on women—two recently released and two older works I was curious to rewatch—to see how the female characters were understood in their time, and to think about who I was when I first saw them. My selections were random, the way you fall upon things in Pandemica, yet weirdly (or tellingly), all the female characters were made to stand for something—a phenomenon, a type, a cautionary example—apart from being a particular person.

Prime Suspect, for instance, which began airing thirty years ago, stars Helen Mirren as London detective Jane Tennison, a character stunningly aware of other people and truly alive only while solving murders. The men on the force sneer and ma'am her to death, including a doughy, improbable boyfriend, who walks out on her because she's too busy chasing a serial killer to cook dinner for him. The show is mesmerizing, partly because of Mirren's stoicism, tenderness, and sexy way of looking people in the eye, and partly because it examines what still goes on—a woman with exceptional ability having to fight against a world that doesn't want her with as much energy as she pursues criminals.

The series comes off dated at times, especially in the extra amount of punishment meted out to Jane, something the creators seem unaware of—showing her frustrated, starved, and denied less because of sexism than because it's how women are understood to exist in the world, fairly or unfairly. Whenever female characters get screwed and screwed again, despite their efforts individually or collectively, it tells the viewer not to worry; the world you woke up in remains intact. I don't think this undermining of a show's own analysis is standard practice anymore, but it was the case for a very long time when I covered film and TV in the eighties and nineties that denying female characters gratification with a sadistic edge—in movies like *Broadcast News* (1987) and *As Good as It Gets* (1997)—was a glaring trend that didn't often get named.

Watching *Prime Suspect*, I kept wondering what it would be like to speak the way Mirren does—softly and with almost no visible emotion. Then I remembered there is freedom in knowing you won't change. The other day the man I live with said, "I probably won't shovel snow in my late eighties." I said, "Why not?"

For no reason I can point to, we watched the Criterion Collection edition of *Darling*, directed by John Schlesinger and with a screenplay by Frederic Raphael. In 1965, when the movie was released, it was something everyone talked about, said to be charting the cynicism of the world and the headlong, icy way modern women went after what they wanted. (They did?) Seeing it now, the question you can't help asking is: Why does Julie Christie wear so many scarves over her bouffant 'do? Julie's character, Diana Scott, is looking for a way to dodge domesticity and get to the party, and her way is through men, which leads back to some house or other, although she doesn't foresee this.

To be honest, the movie did stir memories of the time we all married Italian princes we had had, like, no conversations with and dressed up in gowns to eat alone when our husbands went to Rome to visit Mama. We were bored. So bored. Bored, bored, bored. Everyone adjusted their voices to the clipped, crackly, fake upper-class accent of Audrey Hepburn. Even Julie Christie! We represented the fallen world and the vacuousness of the vacuum that had opened between drab, postwar England and the swinging whatever poking up from the dead land. We girls represented vacuousness in every movie made because that's what we were made to represent. (Maybe not every movie. Don't quote me.) Directors looked at us with distaste and fascination. Obviously.

The best moment in the film: Julie beginning her affair with Dirk Bogarde by sticking a finger in his mouth as he sleeps on a train. Bogarde is beautiful and great to watch. Laurence Harvey, also a love interest in the film, ghouls around, his mouth an unbroken line. And there we were, pacing the ancient stone paths of the castle we'd finally moved into, breaking hearts like the porcelain figurines we smashed to the floor and wondering how in hell we were going to get out of this one. Julie received an Academy Award that year for Best Actress.

The past few days I've been thinking about my teacher Morris Dickstein, who died recently, and who in 1968 taught a seminar on Blake at Columbia University. 1968 is only a few years after 1965, but they might as well have been different eras. The Blake seminar so vibrated with the love Morris felt for the great poet of freedom and rebellion, and with the love he felt for the students who came each week to watch ideas shoot from his forehead, we would never forget the feeling of being there. Everyone in the class moved toward each other. One was Lenny Davis, and in this setting, I think we could foresee that in all the decades to come, we'd find ourselves from time to time at a bar, talking as if it would always be 1968.

In the seminar, we read every word Blake wrote. We were invited to Morris's apartment. It was a time when students and faculty mixed, and if you were a student, you were in awe of everything about your professors. Over the years, I would cross paths with Morris at screenings and book events, and I would always be happy to see him. No one knows the resonances they produce when they teach a class and the class becomes a thing. No one knows these resonances can last nearly a lifetime.

If not for the women's movement—fully up and running by 1968—we might all have become Diana Scotts. I had friends who didn't eat in their apartments as a way to be anorexic. I would open their refrigerators, and there would be leftovers from expensive restaurants I was jealous they'd gone to, and on top of bits of this and that they'd scooped into aluminum tins would grow lovely, mossy topiaries of mold. Because they didn't eat in their apartments.

Watching the four-part documentary *Allen v. Farrow* (2021), the Diana Scott approach to going places floated to mind. The way Mia tucked herself into the lives of men with mastery in their work while remaining insecure about her own: Frank Sinatra, André Previn, Woody Allen. Maybe in the life of every Diana Scott eventually arrives a boyfriend who will marry your daughter.

Farrow's face, bathed in light in the interviews, is still amazed at the way the world works, as if she's remained the perfect late-sixties gamine she played all those years ago in such movies as *Rosemary's Baby* (1968). There's no evidence in her comments of irony or a sense of humor, except for the deadpan delivery of the fact that Previn fell in love with her best friend when she was off making a movie, and how that ended their marriage. Mia doesn't mention she had done the same thing years earlier to Dory Previn when she got together with André, a detail that might have shown viewers she, too, knows that people fuck the people they want to fuck. In a sense, by editing out information, Farrow (and the filmmakers) turn Farrow into a symbol—in this case, Woman Betrayed—so Allen will come across as an especially ruthless liar. They didn't need to.

Allen does that job all by himself, appearing deeply manipulative in footage and interviews, a man who for so long has lived unimpeded in a world of his own making he seems to believe the lies he tells himself about his actions toward his family. Feeling disgust toward him as a person, I was curious to see what I'd think of his work, so I rewatched the "cloning from the nose" sequence in *Sleeper* (1973).

It's hilarious. What can I tell you? With comedy, you laugh/you don't laugh. And if you laugh, you've laughed. The sequence is a Marx Brothers' routine of schmendricks pretending to be experts at something. In this case, Allen and Diane Keaton are fake doctors, claiming they can restore the state's dictator by growing him from his nose, the only remnant left after an explosion. In an operating theater, stalling for time, Keaton lays out the shoes and gloves and pants the dictator will grow into from the nose, and part of the reason this is funny is that we do this all the time: stall before starting a project by loading software we won't need, or sharpening pencils, or cleaning the studio, hoping the project will grow itself from an idea we've jotted on a napkin.

In other news, I regrouted the floor of the upstairs bathroom the serial-killer owners had painted a green so absent of hope plants died there. I painted the walls the pearl gray of a moody ocean sky. The grout was too far gone to clean, so I mixed up fresh grout and went at it. The man I live with came to the door and said, "Did you read the instructions on the box?" I said, "What a good idea. Would you mind letting me know what they say?"

I watched *Nomadland* (2020), Netflix's Oscar-nominated film about a band of people made permanently homeless via the gig economy and maybe some questionable life choices. If you admire the movie, maybe skip this section. I thought the movie was dull. It couldn't find anything interesting in the people it asked us to spend time with, as if having pointed views or talents or interests would subvert the characters' function as symbols.

Symbols of what? Disappointment in their system of government? In the inequities of wealth and opportunities for employment? In the way life ineluctably dwindles to lessness and bewilderment, no matter what you plan or don't plan? Viewing characters as sociological cases insults them and underpins the film's sentimentality. You can hear it in the heart-tugging music and note it in the many times we see main-character Fern cleaning something with a dirty rag.

The movie feels like an essay without a topic, and although Frances McDormand as Fern is fun to watch no matter what she does, she seems angry about having to move from joyless scene to joyless scene. Even the nice-looking food served at the Thanksgiving dinner Fern goes to looks like it wants to kill itself as a way to leave the table.

The interesting thing about Fern is that, apart from economic conditions, we really don't know why any of the things that have happened to her happened to her. The husband is a set of propositions: *I married, we worked, he died.* Nothing of their relationship is revealed—no sense of them together—and then the Shakespeare sonnet she recites meant to carry some ghostly load of meaning it can't.

Fern is shut off from most of the people she interacts with, which seems understandable, given they aren't very compelling. What does she want, other than to avoid people? I don't think she knows, and this, too, is interesting, but the movie doesn't want you to find Fern's lostness in herself interesting. It wants her, again, to stand for a social phenomenon.

At its most intriguing, the movie is a study in truculent aloneness. I liked Fern rejecting a slot in the Thanksgiving family and in her sister's suburban world. But I don't think the movie wants you to see it as a study in truculence. Even if you do see it that way, what does Fern want that she can't get: Enough money to live without dependence on anyone else? Maybe, but then the movie would have had to make a better case for solitude, instead of the tepid one it makes for communality.

Yesterday, I sold the metal stool I'd bought in Arizona for some damn reason and that the man I live with had never liked. A moment ago, another man came to mind, who had caused me pain in love, and I found myself thinking, *I hope you are right now feeling pain in love.* I wondered if I really felt this way. I was far from the heat of that time, yet I could summon the memory if I wanted to. Flies have appeared on the railings surrounding the deck. You spray them with whatever, and a minute later, they return, like resentment.

Bits of glass glint up in the soil above where, last year, we dug out the trash the serial killers had dumped on the land. The plan is to cover them with wood chips. This year, I will accept the plants people offer me and garden again in the I-don't-really-know-how-this-works way I did last year. If I had to know what I was doing before doing it, I wouldn't do anything.

For just this day, the temperatures will reach the sixties, and I feel a stirring without direction. It's like entering an elevator and hearing only part of a story before people get out. Do you have a spare room? Are there ants there? What is the Wi-Fi password? On the road I walk each day, I pass a house owned by a priest I once met who has recently died. I remember the flowers that bloomed there last year: iris, lilies, daffodils, and tulips, and they will bloom again. Already there are buds on the forsythia, and today I saw a cardinal hop along the branch of a tree. On this property is a small house in addition to the regular house, a small house the size of a playhouse with a miniature front porch, and it's painted a shade of blue so dazzling it is unlike anything else on the road. I call it peacock blue, even though I don't know if such a color exists.

HUDSON, New York, June 2020
Part 1

When we could still go out, we didn't shut down anything.
During the years of Trump, there was only one subject, and it was boring because no one had anything insightful to say about how it had happened. All other subjects were irrelevant, and our thinking drifted under a cloud. No one could figure out how to stop the thing that had happened. I don't know why. Let's let it go.

The virus, by comparison, was a relief.
The virus was a different destructive thing to think about. It had no intentions. It didn't produce our passivity. It wasn't even alive. It ushered in the great Pause in which we saw we didn't miss the torpor we'd been living in. We tried not to get sick and die.

I wondered if I had something to say about women and COVID-19.
On May 25, George Floyd, a forty-six-year-old Black

man, was murdered while handcuffed behind his back and prone on a Minneapolis street by white police officer Derek Chauvin, who knelt on his neck for almost nine minutes with the force of his two hundred pounds while Floyd begged for his life, knowing he was being suffocated. Why this piece of racist brutality ended the torpor when stacks of racist killings and other harms at borders and detention camps and on urban streets did not end the torpor will not be known, and it doesn't matter because—as was mentioned earlier—the origin of a thing does not determine its course. The great resistance was launched just when it was most dangerous medically for people to gather, and something about the danger fed the excitement of moving into public space with other bodies you could smell and on whose skin you could see light fall. You need libido to overcome torpor.

Language.
Inside the torpor, people used the words *safe space* a lot. When people talked about wanting *safe spaces*, they weren't thinking about the threat of murder by police. They were saying something like, *Don't do or say something that is going to stir emotions I don't want to feel.* To have emotionally *safe space* means you are going to badger people for disturbing you. You are going to mark them unfit for consumption not only by you but by everyone else. This approach became popular

because people like to tell other people what's best for them. This is a reason dogs are better to hang out with than people.

Speaking of women.
I hate-watched *Mrs. America*, a nine-episode series centered on Phyllis Schlafly. Who? Schlafly, a profoundly uninteresting, dime-a-dozen hater of women, who, in the 1970s, led mainly white Southern women in a campaign to defeat the Equal Rights Amendment. Gloria Steinem told an interviewer for *The Guardian* that Schlafly didn't, in fact, change a single vote in the final defeat of the ERA. Gloria, Bella Abzug, Shirley Chisholm, and other feminists are depicted in the show, but the sum of their screen time barely equals the footage about Schlafly. The feminists are shown squabbling and struggling to learn party politics, as if the ERA's defeat was owing to their incompetence. In a reality I participated in, these women did everything they could to rethink the world. It's crazy to blame women for the hatred of women.

Did women in the second-wave movement need to learn from each other about class and race and sexuality and everything else up for grabs? We did. But that's not the point. The point is that feminists didn't lose what they never had to begin with. The point was and remains that hatred of women is more powerful, better funded, more experienced, meaner, more bitter, more vicious, and more lunatic than opposition to it. It's also loaded with women recruited to look the other way and preserve what they think of as their safety. No one gains status in the world by promoting the rights of women.

I need to say something about the Karen thing flying around. It's difficult to swat back at because it's funny, among other things. A Karen is not only blond and white and a soccer mom, she's an antivaxxer! She's dumb as a stump. And yes, such humans exist. But for fuck's sake, the Karening is also a way to beat up women as the most wickedly clueless racists in the heap, while, in reality, all the stupidity of all the Karens in the world doesn't come close to the homicidal destruction wrought by one Donald. I say this including the 911 call made by Amy Cooper in Central Park against bird watcher Chris Cooper, who captured her on videotape. The issue here was Amy Cooper's racism, not her femaleness, but they got lumped together in coverage of the incident as if her femaleness had produced her racism, and as if damning the racist for being female—she should be better because she's a woman, she should clean up after the horror shows of male racists?—was going to advance the cause of racial justice. How?

HUDSON, New York, June 2020
Part 2

The other day I was planting irises given to me by a friend. We had circled her garden in masks, and after a while, it seemed better to be alone. As I'm planting the irises, I remember riding in the back of a van. In the van, I am seated beside a man—an actor, maybe—uncertain of his future, very handsome and kind in a way I cannot put my finger on. It's late, maybe three in the morning, and the other waiters are sleeping. They are dead tired, and the handsome man and I are touching each other slowly in the rhythm of the ride, and we are kissing. We have worked a party in Westchester or further away, and I don't know why this happens. I'm fifty-four. He's thirtysomething, and the sadness of catering floats around us. During parties, sadness rises off the guests, the sense of a social occasion no one really wants to be at. Kissing the actor quiets something and arouses something—not just desire but something soft and inexplicable, and I know why I'm remembering this in COVID times.

The man I live with says he will dig out the trash in the ravine. He doesn't want the man who helps us to get ticks. The man who helps us has a gentle smile, poor eyesight, and a ZZ Top beard that floats as he strides along. The man I live with tells the man who helps us to find something he feels like doing instead, and the man who helps us trims the lower branches of the spruces that look like dirty petticoats around the legs of the trees. I say to the man I live with, "You'll get ticks." He says, "I'll use the stuff that keeps them off." The stuff that keeps them off is on the floor of the mudroom. We can't keep up with the ways we need to be careful here. I say, "I'll help you dig out the trash," and we climb over mossy rocks into the ravine, and it's like entering a museum. Trees that have grown through twisted barbed wire have keeled over, their roots exposed, like the limbs of accident victims tossed into a common grave. We dig up rusted sardine cans, cobalt-blue bottles of milk of magnesia, the lids of pots, the soles of shoes—all the innards of a life no one was supposed to go looking for.

Last night I learned a friend had died in Rome, and it was like picking up a hose with a wasp on the nozzle—the delay between the sting and your understanding of what has caused it. I had coffee with my friend a year ago in SoHo, at a fancy place with good biscotti. She told me she had received a diagnosis that

— 26 —

made walking difficult. She didn't know how long she would live. She said this without complaint. She had been determined to live an interesting life, far from where she'd started out in rural Pennsylvania, and she'd done that. A few years ago the man I live with and I visited her in Rome, climbing steep steps to get to her apartment. Up and up we went, only to find more steps.

I have been thinking about blood, the idea that the people we are related to are closer to us than the people we meet along the way. I mention blood because I think it's a pitch selling shares in a tribe or clan. Tribes and clans serve the interests of I-don't-know-who, but still, it's a pitch you can't believe in because it's a pitch. The people I've known who are not blood and whom I have loved—oh my god, so much more significant, really, if you add the numbers.

It's evening, and trees are stretching to the sky. I remember a Shiba Inu who was standing by the entrance to my building. He looked up, and I placed my hand on the furrow between his eyes and slowly moved my hand to his ears, then across his long neck and tapered waist, and down to his curled tail. I dreamed I cut off my front tooth and thought I could glue it back with saliva. I could not glue it back with saliva. I remember a man I gave a mug to, as well as a silk shirt and a copy of Baudelaire. After I gave him the shirt, he became better at sex. After he left me, I saw him at a memorial service and wondered if he still had the shirt. He was wearing a suit the color of a peach that was riding up his arms and legs. He looked beautiful, except for the tight suit. If all of life were up to me, I would make one reckless decision after the next and learn nothing.

I watched *Unorthodox* on Netflix, about a nineteen-year-old woman named Esty who escapes to Berlin from Brooklyn and an arranged marriage within the Satmar Hasidic sect. It's based on a memoir by Deborah Feldman. As Esty, Israeli actor Shira Haas is luminous and alert to her surroundings, the way a trained spy is. She's afraid of being captured and pulled back. Plus, she still feels loyal to the post-Holocaust mission of her sect: to keep Jews alive in the world. Almost all the dialogue is in Yiddish, and I loved feeling the language wash over me, the familiarity. I don't know all the words, of course, but this was the language of my mother speaking to my grandmother and her siblings. My mother was born on the Lower East Side and did not learn English until she started school at five. It remained her first language and secret language, spoken with my father, the language of curses and affection, often interchangeable. Here is the thing I want to stress: although Esty must escape a culture that controls and degrades her by rituals and laws, and although the series shows this to us, it does not speak about misogyny directly.

The focus is, instead, on Jews escaping religious confinement in the United States and seeking freedom in Germany, the site, in an earlier time, of their planned extinction. It's as if confronting misogyny within Orthodox religious life might be construed as anti-Semitic, although not naming these practices as human rights violations is the way the larger culture gives a pass to misogyny. By focusing on one woman's plight, the show makes it seem like a personal story instead of a widespread social condition. Esty keeps saying, "I'm strange. I'm not like other women." That's what every woman in cultural lockdown believes.

This morning the man I live with and I were listening to Joni Mitchell sing "A Case of You," and I thought about the lyrics in relationship to #MeToo. I thought about this, even though there is no such thing as a #MeToo philosophy of sex you can nail down. I thought #MeToo doesn't know what to do with the sexual desire of a woman when it's mixed with drunken passion for another person you are lucky to feel even once in a lifetime. That's what the song portrays: the lust felt by a woman for a man.

It's widely known Joni was writing about her love affair with Leonard Cohen. The lyrics that struck me were these:

I met a woman
She had a mouth like yours
She knew your life
She knew your devils and your deeds
And she said, "Go to him, stay with him if you can
But be prepared to bleed"

The woman with a mouth like Leonard's is his mother. So here is a mother—not Joni's, but a woman of an older generation, instructing a younger woman to shape herself around an attractive and difficult man. From our perspective now, you could wonder why Mom doesn't think her son needs to shape himself to fit into Joni's life. In 1971, when the song was written, the women's movement was at full throttle, and plenty of us were thinking these exact thoughts. But Joni wasn't a feminist and has said numerous times she's still not a feminist (fuck her), but put that aside for now.

Back to young Joni and young Leonard. Young Leonard was already a star and very sexy. Not gorgeous—he just had a sexiness that came across in his writing and singing, a man awash in sex in ways women could identify with. I don't know if he was actually good in bed, but never mind. Leonard can probably have sex with anyone he wants whenever he wants to, and what human is going to resist that? (Not a real question.) The thing I love about this song and this lyric is that Joni/the narrator doesn't care about getting wounded. She's "prepared to bleed" because in these kinds of encounters, we always have to be prepared to bleed. The thrill is no safety because there is nothing less safe than safety. This is what the song is about.

HUDSON, New York, July 22, 2020

I am remembering a day I walked along Halsey Street
in Brooklyn. Halsey Street is lined with townhouses
in various states of disrepair. I walked past a park with
patchy lawns, then through a section where men—it
was mostly men—were cooking on grills and laughing
and listening to jazz and drinking beer. A man was
burning incense. He was tall and burly. I said, "That
smells great." He said, "It's called Barack Obama."
There was a gap between his front teeth, and they were
capped in gold. I said, "Oh, you are making me cry."
He said, "Don't cry. Pray for him. He's a good man."
I said I would. I don't pray. He said, "Would you like
some incense?" I said, "Thank you. I'm going to a bar."

It's hot, and there isn't enough rain. In Beckett's plays,
first there are carrots and turnips, and then only turnips. First you are buried up to your waist, then you
are buried up to your neck. The birds are singing as if
everything's great. In the 1960s and 1970s, when we
used phrases like "social transformation," we didn't

know the extent to which trillionaires controlled things. The truth of my life is I was always going to miss a lot of what's going on.

I bought a pot roast to grill as a steak. The man I live with is reading Foucault's last lectures on telling the truth about yourself. We attached Tiki lamps we found in the garden shed to the railings of the deck, and we are burning citronella oil to ward off mosquitoes. The place looks like Don Ho's. If you come here, I will serve you a cocktail with a small umbrella in it.

Last night, we watched *Roma* on Netflix, a film by Alfonso Cuarón, set in the Mexico City of his youth. It's an ode to the woman who worked for the bourgeois household he grew up in. She's called Cleo in the film, and we see her from morning till night, gathering laundry, making beds, setting out meals, sweeping up dog shit, and hosing down a long driveway too narrow for the cars that scrape against the walls.

The camera sees the world through her eyes, and at the same time looks almost exclusively at her expressive face, its secrets racing behind her brow. What matters to her, from moment to moment, matters to us, as she shuttles between Spanish and Mixtec, the indigenous language of the village where she's from. The family and its travails is the *Hamlet* we glimpse from time to time while our Rosencranz or Guildenstern gets pregnant, carries on schlepping, gives birth to a stillborn baby, feels relieved and guilty that she can again dream of a larger life, and saves two children from drowning, although she cannot swim. The film sometimes reminded me of *Jeanne Dielman*, Chantal Akerman's detailed meditation on a woman who turns tricks in her living room to make ends meet. Cuarón's extraordinary camera moves so slowly over Cleo's world, there is time to think about the potentials of life, as well as its emptiness.

I visited the house of a friend, and we sat outside on wooden chairs, watching a thundercloud approach like a large, rolled carpet. You could see rain in the distance, smudging the chalky sky underneath. She gave me a bowl of potato chips while she ate wedges of raw cabbage. It amazes me when people stretch toward self-improvement. Really, we like our sloppy, unhappy lives just fine.

My friend looked pretty in the dim light. We were women who had fashioned a look somewhere along the line and expected to retain it until the universe expanded and we were swallowed by darkness.

I found postcards my mother had sent me at camp. She said, "I miss you. I can't wait for you to come home." And I could see her standing alone in the back of our little house in Long Beach, staring past the flag-stone patio to a giant green hedge.

My sister died three years ago yesterday. Last night I dreamed the man I live with told a room full of people Donald Trump was dead, and I was the only one who cheered. Yesterday I asked him to explain a friend who was behaving mostly dry, like the weather, with an occasional sprinkle of grief he lets fall on people. He said, "No one knows why anyone does anything, including the person who is doing the thing. We remain a mystery, and then we die." I found this consoling and asked him to hold me as I bent back in the tiniest, lamest backbend you will ever see. It cured all my ailments. Along a roadside, I dug up a clump of wild rose, soaked the roots in a tub of water for several days, and planted it in the front yard. Most of the branches turned brown, but a few spindly ones retained their leaves, and after some time one of the tiny branches sprouted new leaves. It was thrilling.

HUDSON, New York, September 2020

I saw the face of a friend at a Zoom event for beloved feminist Ann Snitow. She had died the year before, and people were gathering to miss her and think about her life. I was happy to see the face of the friend on Zoom and wrote to tell her, and we exchanged a few remarks on Facebook Messenger, agreeing to speak on the phone.

Today in the bath I thought with distaste about abstract nouns such as *conflict* and *abuse*, although I like the phrase coined by Sarah Schulman that is also the title of a book she wrote, *Conflict Is Not Abuse*. In the bath, I imagined Sarah Schulman addressing the twentysomethings she teaches, and I saw her telling them to chill in the face of remarks they don't like. I saw her telling them not to see language as harming them and not to shun things they felt impinged on what they considered their safety. Sarah Schulman could have meant something different because abstract language doesn't mean anything concrete. The word *conflict* doesn't mean anything concrete, and the word *abuse* doesn't mean anything concrete, even with examples. When I hear words that are not concrete used as if they convey a world of shared understanding, I tell everyone how much this bugs me. I doubt they care.

I wrote to the friend I saw on Zoom, saying I thought we'd first met at a party thrown in the giant apartment on West End Avenue, where Nanette Ranone lived in a commune with Gwenda Blair and others. They were young women on the move with power in the world. They were feminists, thinking about feminism in ways that were similar and ways that maybe were not. The friend I saw on Zoom was younger than me, and I remembered thinking she was beautiful with almond eyes and a face like some kind of slinky animal. She was ambitious. Maybe she was already writing for *The Village Voice*, where I, too, wrote. Maybe I had come to the party with Vivian Gornick, who knew all the feminists in the world at that point.

I was in my early thirties. The friend I saw on Zoom recalled having interviewed Vivian on one occasion. She saw herself as a journalist. She was on an errand to improve the world, not only for women but for all people under some boot. She was fierce and I was a little afraid of her, as I am of all women who seem to know where they are going.

If you are part of a movement for social change, you are going to hear abstract language, and if you go around questioning it, people are going to hate you, and you will feel like the outsider you always make yourself into. You will ask yourself why you can't go along, why you can't get along, why you wind up being disloyal or being considered disloyal for slipping another wedge of thought onto the table, like a piece of cheese no one else is going to eat.

Recently I was a presenter at two other Zoom events, and at both events women in the audience asked why women tear each other down. They said women are competitive, echoing a notion popular among people who don't like women. I said at one of the Zoom events, "Women dislike women as much as everyone else does." I was thinking about something I didn't say, which is that women find it easier to fight for the liberation of people who aren't women than to fight for the liberation of women as a group that is discriminated against for being women. It feels selfish to them. God forbid a woman should think about the interests of women first or at all. At the second Zoom event, a woman who is a feminist told the woman who asked about women fighting with each other that women are a million times nicer to women than men are to women. She said women help each other all the time, are supportive, look out for each other—which is also true.

In the 1960s, when I entered the women's movement, everyone had her own private feminism, and some people, like Ann Snitow, could work in worlds foreign to them. Ann forged alliances with women who considered themselves feminists and didn't necessarily share her sense of what that was. A belief no matter what in abortion rights? Not everyone who calls herself a feminist believes this. To me, anyone who doesn't champion the right of women to abortion isn't a feminist, but I'm not the one you send out to make common cause amid a sea of conflict. There are women who call themselves feminists and don't concern themselves with sexism and misogyny. Some of these women believe in God and in religions that restrict the mobility of women in public and private space. To rummage around for even five minutes in practices that harm and constrict women and also hold on to the tenets of your religion will blow off the top of your head.

At the Zoom event for Ann, listening to women recall Ann's service to women's liberation and to them personally, as I listened to how large a life in love and friendship she'd made, how accepting and at the same time sharp-minded she was, as I listened and remembered, I felt alienated, as I always do in groups, comparing her large accomplishments to my measly ones, comparing my knowledge of Ann, which wasn't deep or probably very important to her, to her intimacy with others. One of those others was the friend I was happy to see. I watched her face throughout the testimonies and thought maybe she felt out of it, too, because no one is interesting when they speak abstractly, and most of the people used the language of summary and analysis to describe what they did, what they loved, what they remembered.

That's when I slipped back to the party at the giant apartment of Nanette Ranone, how I had marveled at such a place with so many rooms and women living together with lovers and children and conflict. How could there not be conflict, and how could women not want to help each other through our beautiful, awkward lives? I missed the sense of being on the lip of things about to unfold: the large and small details of female existence, how we talk to each other, how we can't wait to tell each other what we are doing and thinking about, how we take each other's faces in our hands. Nothing is more interesting, not really, if you wake us suddenly in the middle of the night and say, "Who are you? What happened to you along the way?"

HUDSON, New York, September 29, 2020

The characters in Beckett's plays blurt things out in a way that seems random. Enough disconnected blurts, and a world forms. Here we are: intimate, anonymous, in love with each other, dead. The erotic jolt of certain words still amazes me.

Yesterday I ate two kinds of cake. At the dump, an attendant lifted my bags of recyclables from the car. I said, "Do you need help?" He said, "Not unless you're a shrink." A friend on Facebook said it was Yom Kippur and he was fasting. He wanted to know what kinds of cake I'd eaten. I said, "Frozen cheesecake from Sara Lee and frozen lemon layer cake from Pepperidge Farm." His interest stirred my cold, dark heart.

People don't give away power. They may feel an obligation to do it, but then they don't do it. Change happens through boredom. Change happens when people with power become bored with the things power has given them. It's the same as falling out of love. They just don't care anymore about being the thing they thought they were supposed to be. Suddenly, other kinds of people look interesting, look creative, look important—or at least new.

It's hot again after a few weeks of autumnal briskness. A golden rudbeckia is poking up over the railing of the deck. The tomatoes are beginning to pack it in. The smell of their leaves is fading, even on the vine. Who knew? We drove to Hudson to pick up strips for the man I live with to test the sugar in his blood. On the way back, we passed a chair on the road. I thought it might be the kind of lawn chair I am always looking for, with a frame of bent metal. It took everything in the man I live with to turn the car around. The chair was white and made of plastic with a mesh seat, and at first, I thought, "Oh no, too ugly." Then I pictured it in the backyard, covered with colorful cushions, and I loaded it into the car.

At home, it looked like a broken tooth in an otherwise rosy mouth. I placed it near the stone patio. No, completely awful. I placed it on a hill and tried sitting in it. It was low to the ground, a chair you would be placed in during an interrogation in a hostage situation.

I went inside to cook, and what was staring back at me through the kitchen window? The chair was more starkly white than before, a glowing, poisonous white against the grass, electrified from hours of rain. Never did the backyard's fanciful birdbath and flower-stand stumps stand out in more touching relief than against the grotesque chair. I moved it to the back of the house, which was desperately untended. Nothing had been planted. You could see the cinder-block foundation, and still it was degraded by the hideous chair.

I grabbed the chair and carried it to the road. The man I live with made a sign that said FREE. Poor chair. No sooner rescued than again abandoned.

Now that Ruth Bader Ginsberg has died, people proclaim we will lose our right to abortion—as if, a little bit, they want the worst to happen. I wish they would stop it. Just fucking stop it. I can count on the fingers of one hand the men I have known over the many years I have been observing the world's distaste for women, the number of men who have fought shoulder to shoulder with women to secure women's right to have abortions. The left-wing men I have known have fought for the rights of gay people and trans people. Included in these categories are male humans. Men. Fighting for men is not so hard. They don't have to stoop to do it. But to sign up for the rights of women and girls, a category that in their minds does not include them, is to sign up, in effect, to fight on the girls' team and thus feel something slippery in the gut, unselved and fishy, not required, not in my backyard. How many men now, reading these words (ha!), can say they have stood on a picket line or protested specifically for the right of a woman to have an abortion? What's your plan, men, if this prediction of doom proves correct? Will it still be *our* problem?

Last night I was awakened by the smell of skunk. I smelled skunk in my dream and in the bedroom when I opened my eyes. I whispered in the ear of the man I live with, "Are you awake?" He said, "I am now." I said, "I smell skunk." He said, "I don't smell it." He went downstairs. When he came back, I said, "Did you think it might be on the porch?" He said, "No. There is no skunk." I said, "Do you smell it now?" He said, "No." We went back to sleep, and when we got up, the smell was gone. The man I live with said, "You dreamed the smell." I said, "Can a dream smell linger when you aren't dreaming?" He said, "Apparently." He opened his closet and said, "It smells funny in here." I went in. It didn't smell any funnier than usual. I said, "If there was a skunk in your closet, you'd know it." He said, "A wasp is crawling on the window. Do you think it's inside or outside?"

I once admired a pair of ankle boots worn by Melania Trump, but I was afraid to mention this to anyone. These days, everyone will have fifteen minutes when they are savagely denounced on social media. Squirrels have invaded the bird feeders. I don't care. A tomato has fifty million seeds (more or less), any one of which will make a tomato plant that will yield a million tomatoes (more or less). It's the absence of scheme, motive, justification, blame, judgment, and categorical thinking I love. The unexamined life is worth living.

No one is willing to say Melania is beautiful because they hate her. They mention her 1980s TJ Maxx fashion bent that must give her enormous personal pleasure, or else how could she? In most photographs, she wears a terrified, frozen expression, but she's beautiful, and I'm always surprised by her slanting eyes and wide cheekbones. Many very ugly people, Donald Trump among them, wear their inner decay on the outside. With Melania, there is a disconnect between what she looks like and what she is. Inconsistency is her great gift to us.

The past few nights, we streamed *Away* on Netflix, starring Hilary Swank as an astronaut with a toothy smile and zero sex appeal. Sorry. What can I tell you? Josh Charles plays her husband. Josh Charles, who played Will Gardner on *The Good Wife*, a sexy man who isn't terribly good-looking with his jutting beak of a nose, and he's not as slender as before. It doesn't matter.

Hilary leaves her daughter, a teenager, and her husband to fly to the moon and then to Mars, a trip lasting three years, in the company of Mark Ivanir, the Russian actor who was snarly and aggressive in *Homeland* and who is snarly and aggressive here. You can tell he misses playing opposite Mandy Patinkin, the same way Josh Charles misses playing opposite Julianna Margulies and Archie Panjabi. How did Hilary get the part? Her career is perplexing, like a further-neutered Jodi Foster. I don't think she looks that great in a space helmet, which is a little like a face filling a TV screen.

Before the blastoff to Mars, Hilary learns that Josh Charles has had a stroke as a consequence of a congenital illness, and Hilary's daughter pleads with her to come back and ditch being the commander of the Mars mission. Mom says she will, and then the chief of NASA, a woman, pleads with Hilary to continue the mission or she will set back the liberation of women by decades. And Hilary snaps, "Don't give me any of your feminist bullshit," and you think this is meant to show us that deep down, Hilary is the kind of girl you can look up at in the sky and believe is risking her life for a calling higher than the truth of personal pleasure and a wish to get out of the house.

I keep imagining how great it would be to leave this planet, which has become like a single bloated body we're all attached to. You can't go anywhere on Earth and forget Trump. The people who love him want a world that is ruined because . . . it was always ruined for them? No one knows why anyone does anything (as has been mentioned). There's a scene in the Mars show when one of the astronauts removes a sock and a piece of his heel comes away from his foot and floats up to his face, and he looks at it with horror. That's the way we look just about all the time, seeing the distance we've come from our lives in the Before. I mean the Before without Trump.

I've been noticing a false note about suffering on social media that's probably a thing elsewhere and maybe not a new thing, but I don't go to elsewhere much these days. So many people are suffering, and they want their suffering to mean something, and the thing I've noticed is a tendency to convert suffering into an opportunity for growth or something like that—to convert suffering into a life experience and say the terrible thing that is happening to them is teaching them something and enlarging their lives. To set themselves up as a model for others to follow? To believe nothing bad is all bad? I don't want to hurt the feelings of anyone portraying their suffering this way, but it comes off like another formula for rightfeeling and coercive positivity. If I were undergoing one of these ordeals, I wouldn't believe a word of what they're saying.

In contrast, I am thinking about two books that look at suffering as a subject, rather than as an occasion for uplift: Jacobo Timerman's *Prisoner Without a Name, Cell Without a Number* (1981), a memoir of his imprisonment and torture as a journalist in Argentina, and Lucy Grealy's *Autobiography of a Face* (2003), a memoir of facial deformity as a consequence of Ewing's sarcoma of the jaw. In both books, the narrators do not say their experiences hurt. They describe their experiences in such sharp detail, the reader feels the pain and the conditions pain arouses, both social and psychological. The authors don't view suffering as a school with information an individual needs to get through life. Suffering teaches nothing, in their view—as, of course, anyone who has suffered knows.

I miss the dead. Even the dead I did not miss when they were alive. The light is beautiful, fading into the trees that soar into the air. People on bikes and on foot wave as they pass the house. Even drivers wave from cars. I wave back. We're saying, "I see you," the way the Boy in *Waiting for Godot* each day assures Gogo and Didi they exist.

Stanley Crouch, the jazz critic and author of *Notes of a Hanging Judge* and *The All-American Skin Game* (among many other books), died the other day. We hadn't been in touch much the past few years. I'd heard he was sick. I don't know from what. I felt sad and shocked by the news. I always liked him. We got along. I don't know why. People like you, and you think, Okay, I like you too. The biggest smile when we greeted each other at *The Village Voice*. He liked me and the writer Paul Berman (*Terror and Liberalism*) in some special way. He liked that we were Jews. He thought there was such a thing as a Jewish writer. I don't, but it made me smile, the way he thought this, and he could have explained and maybe he tried to on more than one occasion before I said, "What are you talking about?" I think what he liked about me and Paul was the shape of our sentences. Their smell, their roundness. Paul wrote sentences from the heart with clarity and sudden swerves to generosity—for example, on the writer Joe Wood: "He was a sensitive essayist with an easy way of speaking in the first person and a frank approach to problems of the American racial situation—an essayist in Baldwin's style, perhaps." Stanley had so much confidence. I had the desire to do the things I was doing. Paul knew a lot. I had feminism, the logic of this analysis that was at the ready and unassailable. I think Stanley got that, or maybe he just liked the look of me looking at his face. Stanley, I'm so sad you have died.

On the phone the other day, a friend asked if there was a future, and I said there was a future with a narrative that has been broken. It's good this narrative has been broken. In the narrative that has been broken, people ignored the way so many things they wanted required the suffering of others.

I don't know why something goes right or wrong in the garden. I fail and succeed in the dark. It will be absurd to pot and maintain as many plants as I will try to save over the winter, but I will try to save them. I miss drinking in a bar and riding the subway. I feel I know you, although I've never met you. The wind is rustling.

HUDSON, New York, October 23, 2020

A few days ago, after *New Yorker* writer Jeffrey Toobin accidentally exposed his penis on a Zoom meeting, lots of women I know fumed against him on social media. They saw him as a bad man and his actions bad for women. Apparently, while in a meeting with office colleagues, Toobin was masturbating to something on another screen and thought he had switched himself out of the office meeting. His colleagues saw his penis for a few seconds, and he was mortified. It was an accident. He was not trying to flash them or masturbate in front of them as a turn-on.

I just reread this paragraph again and laughed. Suddenly, a penis when you least expect one. Pants open. It's funny.

The women on social media—some men, too, but I don't care what the men said—saw a chain of incidents in Toobin's life that led to this moment and affirmed his badness. He was masturbating when he should have been doing something else. He had conducted an affair with a younger woman while married. The woman had gotten pregnant. Toobin had made it clear he didn't want parental responsibility for the child and offered to pay for an abortion. The woman had had the baby anyway, then sued him for child support. It was rumored through so-and-so he was a predator and, in one online account, followed a woman into a public bathroom and said he wanted to fist her. He had not supported Hillary Clinton and instead had dogged her for using a private email server for official correspondence while secretary of state.

Women like me, who were interested in the categories of outrage against Toobin, were called defenders of his actions and called this because, as women, we had been trained to give a woman-pass to misbehaving bros, while we would give no such support, it was claimed, to our sister hooligans. Many women hated Toobin because, they said, if a woman had exposed her genitals during a meeting, more hell than could be imagined would have rained down on her, plus no one would come to her defense. The same women also declared that no woman would ever be caught in such a situation because they had better control over their carnal impulses than men did, or because they had more respect for their colleagues than Toobin did. Women had more respect for their colleagues because they were more high-minded, more considerate, more concerned about not losing their jobs—just better humans, owing either to their individual betterness or to being female or to being more distant from their own libido, which endowed them in some unstated way with betterness. Rather than wishing no one be punished for showing their genitals by accident (or on purpose) to other people—showing their genitals, a part of the human body, not rubbing them on unsuspecting passersby—rather than encouraging this freedom, a thing feminists would gain from in that their bodies are forever managed and reviled, the women who hated Toobin wanted him to be fired and felt he had forfeited his credibility as a journalist.

I've never met Toobin. I might not like him if I did. I might get one of those vibes of aversion you get with some people. I think he's a shit for not supporting Hillary. He's very condescending and smug in his writing. And this has nothing to do with thinking about his actions in the Zoom meeting.

Again, he didn't mean to masturbate in public. Masturbating is not a sign you will fail as a colleague or a partner. Having sex outside marriage does not mean you are a bad person. (Marriage probably isn't a good idea. It's a terrible idea, actually.) If you have the child of a man who has made it clear he does not want to be the father of that child, you do not hold the moral high ground when you sue the man for child support. Saying a woman caught accidentally masturbating during a work meeting on Zoom would arouse harder social fire than a man, while probably true, is different from saying a woman ipso facto would not find herself in such a position, which cannot categorically be true and suggests that women are less prone to carnal appetites than men are, which is false. Women as a group may be more careful about getting caught, owing to the sexual double standard where women are judged more harshly than men for the same behaviors. Trying to parse the acts of men under moral fire because you want to understand the categories of reproach that have been heaped on them—to see if there is anything more to them than personal repugnance—does not mean you are giving a woman-pass to a man because he's a man.

Bodies and body parts—let's think about these things. The female body in public space: Who decides where it may move, if it can move at all unescorted in the world? The queer body. The swish body. The trans body. The Black body. Who will allow these bodies to exist without harm? We have fought and fought and fought for this beautiful right. How can it even be a right? A mollusk, a horse. Bodies in the world as they are.

The sexual body in public space. There is no such thing as a body that is not also a sexual body. The nude body covered in order to enter public space. Topless men okay on the street; topless women not okay. Because they're women. Because they're women, the emptiness of the phrase that lit the fuse for the women's movement.

Sex and physical freedom that are not assaultive, not violent, not aggressive—let's focus on these things now. *Aggression* and *coercion* exist in categories separate from *sex* and *nudity*. If they don't in your mind, why not? If, as women, we don't think with reason about sex, desire, mistakes, freedom, and the harms men do to women because, as men, they can get away with it, we duplicate the muddy thinking that justifies keeping us down. There is no way to control the male body without endangering the right of women to move in the world without permission.

To review: A man who may be a dick for reasons publicly known and unknown, who accidentally shows his penis to a group of professional colleagues, is not a dick because he accidentally showed his penis. He is not a dick because he was masturbating. Everyone masturbates, or they are wasting their lives. He is not a dick because he was thinking about sex while thinking about other things as well. This is known as ordinary existence. The penis unwrapped is not ipso facto a thing that needs to be escorted off the premises. It's a body part, a tube of flesh that can look beautiful or like a small turtle head pulled back into its shell. The incident is funny. Mistakes are funny. If you want to see this guy punished, what is his offense?

HUDSON, New York, October 30, 2020

Yesterday, we drove to New York City for the first time since the morning of March 6th. It was a Friday, and I had poison ivy. In the apartment, I saw I'd left a small heater by the couch. It must have been cold. Who were we?

We were in the city to have our teeth cleaned, our dentist is still here. We went in together and left together, and afterward walked a little downtown, and although it is a part of the city I have always loved, I did not feel love. Everything was familiar, except me.

We have been watching *2001: A Space Odyssey*, and we keep falling asleep. I love the boring, retro pace. Everything about it is beautiful and tedious and poignant in the way it captures a future that was already defunct in 1968, when the movie was made. A little while ago, I was chopping vegetables and I thought about an impetuous message I'd sent a friend earlier and worried it might not be welcome, since he hadn't responded. Then a voice in my head said, Say what you would say if you thought you would soon be dead.

An old friend suggested I would be happier if I made the most annoying person in my life into my *teacher*. That was her word. She said I could learn patience, compassion, and a way to drain anger from my life. I felt like I was in a supermarket and my cart was being filled with things I don't eat. Finding instruction in irritation is like faking an orgasm. Then it struck me: I might be the most annoying person in my friend's life, and immediately I felt compassion for her for sticking it out with me all these years.

In the apartment, we sorted mail and gathered things to take back to Hudson. Some things, I'd thought about ahead. Some things, I forgot to take as I floated around, like my good knives. I'd been careful the past year not to rob the apartment for the house. Now I didn't care. "The next time we come, let's take Gardner's coffee table," I said. "We'll put something else there." I didn't know what.

Today, I was a guest on Zoom in the class of a friend, and there they were, twenty bright and beautiful faces, and I asked them to unmute unless there was an owl or a coyote in their apartment so we could feel we were together, where you hear what people are murmuring as well as what others are saying. They had read some work of mine, but really, we wanted to have a conversation about whatever was on their minds in Pandemica. They were tender toward each other and already brilliant, some of them, about the contingent nature of identity, how it was sliding into the next shape you could use as a reference point to find more comfort or freedom for the time you needed it. I felt so happy because I was meeting all these strangers, and it reminded me of riding the subway, when you see the faces of people from everywhere on the planet, and I missed the way you suddenly fall into conversations on the street, and everyone on Zoom nodded—each in a solitary box, missing strangeness, too—and I cried a little, and no one cared.

On Sunday, I will arrive at the age my father was when he died. It seemed old then. I was thirty-five. He fell off a ladder; that was the way he learned he had cancer of the liver. I see him on a ledge outside the hospital. It's summer. The sun is shining on his face for the last time. I'm with him when he dies. Just me, as if we are having a secret affair.

The other night I watched *Let Them All Talk* after the man I live with went to bed. Meryl Streep plays a literary author who invites two college friends (Candice Bergen and Dianne Wiest) on an ocean liner crossing to England so she can accept a prize and steal from their lives for a novel she is writing that has stalled. For the imperious and clueless author, Streep repurposes her *Devil Wears Prada* icy whisper. By now, earlier performances are a prop trunk she rummages in. It's a pointless movie no one looks like they had fun making. We might as well be watching *Old Acquaintance* (1943) with Bette Davis (serious author without man) and Miriam Hopkins (pulp writer with husband). Candy Bergen, playing a man hunter down on her luck, has come on the cruise to exact reparations. Thirty-five years earlier, Meryl had used intimate details confided to her for a novel that wound up costing Candy her marriage. The old college friends do not like each other, and there's no sense they ever did. Never mind. I identified with the writer who steals other people's stories, and that's the reason the movie has stuck with me. Streep feels okay getting away with murder, and you wonder if such a person could write even one sentence that anyone would want to read.

Recently, I ate a whole marijuana gummy not knowing it should have been a quarter, and my thoughts melted at the edges. I remembered a yoga teacher who was loved for his sadism, the way everyone is. My hair was cropped in the style of a man. My fingers were dirty and loose in your mouth. I remembered the smile of

Richard Nixon that looked like a rock had come down hard on his hand. I was the only one onstage who had not learned their lines.

I'll be your Jew. That's how I read Sacha Baron Cohen. Monied, educated, and English, but still a Jew in that world. The world of Virginia Woolf's casual, de rigueur anti-Semitic quips and Orwell's nasty spittle. The Jew in England: Shylock and Fagan. The nose, the hands greasy from counting money. Above all, vulgar, out of it socially. Big gestures. Hands and voice. Vulgar in the extreme, and they seem to enjoy it, they seem not to understand how repulsive the rest of us find them. Cohen's response: You want to see the Jew you secretly harbor in your thoughts, the Jew you no longer dare to speak about publicly—I'll be your Jew, and in being your Jew, I will show you who you are. He's fearless because of his class and accent—also, his tall, handsome man self. Go baby, be their Jew and our reckless vulgarian. There is so much pleasure in what is understood as vulgarity. Another word for this is comedy.

The day after my birthday I found myself thinking about André Glaz, the psychoanalyst who treated several members of my family in the 1960s and when I was fourteen took me into his bed. Thinking about André is a way of missing my sister and a cousin, whom André also took into his bed—in her case, for many years. When I met her again a few years ago, she said, "André shaped my life." I said, "Mine too." We didn't mean the same thing. It was true nonetheless, what each of us said.

André is what happens to a family at some point or other and what separates you from the self you were before. It could be a brother waking up to find himself transformed into a large beetle, or your father being arrested for insider trading while you and your mother stand on the velvet lawn, surprised and not surprised to see him cuffed and carted away.

When I agreed with my cousin that André shaped my life, I was thinking about sex. Yesterday, I heard from someone I had felt an enormous attraction to in the past—one of those weather conditions that makes it impossible to stand up—and I loved the memory of that excitement, and that such sensations exist. The thing about André is he didn't make sex weirder (in a not-good way) than it might have been, had he not entered my life. By fourteen, I was already the sexual creature I was going to be.

Stuff happens to people that is far more marking than what happened to me with him. Far more marking stuff happened to my cousin. That kind of radical shift in the notion of trust and what is true and not true and what can be said and what cannot be said because it just can't be said, and also you are closed off from language for it—that kind of experience will remain on you. Do not think it will ever be small or shadowy or smudged. The way, also, that a marking experience is not everything, is interesting. The way it is possible to know you were not specific in the activity that shaped your life does not prepare you for other times in sexual situations you will not be specific to the person you have fallen for or who has fallen for you, the way the other person will not be specific to you but rather a type from a menu, or the scratch for an itch. The thing that happened with André did not prepare me for life, and yet all that nonspecificity has rolled over my life, as it has everyone's, a series of sporadic, ineluctable tides. They are not functions of cause-and-effect. They coexist with us, and we make of their proximity what we will.

The other morning, I checked to see if my mail-in vote had been counted, and happy day, it had! Then I recapped the last episode of *The Queen's Gambit* for the man I live with. We were in bed, drinking tea. I said at the end, the protagonist, a teenage girl chess prodigy, is alone with a group of old Russian men, who sit outside in Moscow, playing chess at café tables. She's wearing chic '60s clothes, peering at them with her wide, alien eyes and cheekbones that look like

Ping-Pong balls have been inserted under her skin. I could hardly get out a word, I was crying so hard. I said, "She has to stay away from booze and pills before playing the Russian champion for the third time." A curtain of tears fell. The Russian calls an adjournment, and she has time to strategize the game going forward.

In her hotel room, the phone rings, and it's her boyfriend of sorts, who has gathered all the best chess minds to help her game the moves. Now, I'm doubled over with tears. Because she's not alone? Because her extraordinary focus has earned her support? She doesn't need them for the game, of course. I can't stop crying, and I'm sad when there's nothing more to narrate and cry about.

Who is this girl to me? Every girl who ever wanted something? I remember the thrill of centrifugal force on the fast-spinning Tilt-A-Whirl ride. It was like an orgasm building in its wavelike way before I knew what an orgasm was. Again, do it again. The show is set in the time I knew André.

I cut flowers at the farm where we have a share for vegetables. They were the last flowers of the season. Snapdragons, asters, zinnias, still poking up. The cosmos are gone. There were a few last week. Back home, the cosmos I planted late are blooming, and it's like the last child at the circus, with the tents empty and the canvas flaps flying. On the tote bag I was loading the flowers into was a fat black bee looking dazed, out for a ride. We were alone in the field, and rain was coming down hard. I gently nudged the bee to the ground and looked at him or her or it or they or for fuck's sake, I looked at this particular bee that doesn't live in a hive, I learned on Monty Don's *Gardeners' World*. Most bees—most of the great pollinators of earth—are solitary creatures, basically homeless and without roommates, and seem sleepy compared to honeybees and bumblebees because they spend so much time looking for a kip. The bee looked up, and I said, "Goodbye." I said, "Really, you can't go where I'm going. No one can."

HUDSON, New York, November 2020

— 1 —

I walked in a park with hedges cut in the shape of lizards. The clouds looked like my mother. No one is to blame.

I offered water to a man, and he undressed. He said, "'Arbeit macht frei,' you believe that." I said, "Not in the Auschwitz way." He said, "No, you actually believe it." I said, "Some things that can kill you are not interesting." Then it occurred to me: everything that can kill you is uninteresting.

I saw a child drop a lollipop into a coffin. She looked back at the lollipop, surprised she'd let it go. Joan Didion said, "Writers are always selling somebody out."

In Dorset, there were fossils everywhere, except where we walked. It was the same with the rain. What was

I talking about? My sister said, "You look like Mom. I look like Dad. See the little hook at the end of my nose?" I said, "I have a little hook at the end of my nose." Did I?

— 2 —

January 24, 1995. Yesterday, the dog could eat only a few meatballs from my hand. His breathing was slow, and he could not hold up his head. This morning, I took him downstairs and he tried to shake out his fur. I held him as he peed, then scooped him back up and tried to make him comfortable upstairs.

He would not drink water. His kidneys were failing. I settled him on his bed and he lay there, looking as he always did, his head curved over his front paws, his back legs swung to the side. Every half hour or so, he barked weakly in pain.

A few hours later, I laced up my shoes and cried. I held the dog against my chest and kissed the top of his head. It had a furry, soft, summer smell.

Outside, the air was cold and clear. In my arms, he was a bundle splayed this way and that. His head lolled. Halfway to the vet, I felt his body go into a spasm, and by the time I walked through the door, he was unconscious. His eyes were unresponsive. His tongue was hanging out thickly.

He had no blood pressure, but I didn't think he was all the way dead. When someone dies, a shape lifts off. The vet was out with flu, and I asked his assistant to sedate the dog, in case he felt pain. It was difficult for her to find a vein.

His heart stopped, and I stayed with him for a while in the new emptiness. So many times a day, I expect to see him on the couch. I calculate when to walk him and how far.

I had been good to the dog because I loved him. He had been good to me because it was his nature. He would stay still in my arms for hours. There are hardly any dog hairs on the furniture.

— 3 —

Two girls from high school died young. There were only twenty of us in the class. One girl killed herself in her thirties. The other girl died of cancer in her forties. When I heard about these deaths, the girls stood out in relief.

One day, as my mother and I were leaving the circus, swept along on a tide of humanity, I saw a woman grab a glittery doll away from her little girl and throw it in the trash. I started to cry. My mother said, "Why are you crying? It's not happening to you." But it seemed it was.

The girl who killed herself and I had been friends. I could see she was suffering, and it attracted me. She was sexy and dark-haired and very thin. She had grown thinner each year of high school. Her skin was translucent. You could see her blue veins showing through, even on her young cheeks. We didn't have the word *anorexia* then, or the understanding of this kind of starving. I wanted to be thin. She had a high-strung, hectic manner. I was shopping around for a way to be.

— 4 —

Yesterday, on Facebook, I wrote about *The Undoing* and mentioned that Nicole Kidman couldn't tighten her lips in an emotional response because they were already tight from plastic surgery. People jumped on Kidman for having cosmetic surgery. They jumped on cosmetic procedures in general, and I thought: Oh shit, oh shit, I've encouraged these people.

Today I want to tell you how much I love cosmetic procedures. I am 104 years old and as agile as a baby lamb because cosmetic procedures have given me the will to live. I have not had fillers or Botox in what now must be getting onto a year. If COVID doesn't kill me, Zoom will. The man I live with looks good and has done nothing technological to enhance his body and face, unless you count pulling up four thousand tree stumps, which I do count.

In episode four of *The Undoing*, Hugh Grant goes on TV and says, "I'm grieving. I lost someone I love." He means the woman he may have murdered, played by Matilda De Angelis. Hugh's mouth twists to show sadness, and it's grotesque because it's something we haven't seen him do before. Do I want to know who did it, or do I want not to know and think longer about how people lie? I am a little in love with the show for making plot important. With plot, you need a gun, a bludgeoned head, a neon sign reflected in a pool of blood. I wish there were more scenes with Matilda and Nicole kissing. Matilda has some look of intensity about her. Hugh has grown lovely at being a snake in the years following his roles as a beauty with fake sincerity. In certain lights, his face looks like a plate of crepes. Donald Sutherland's eyebrows shadow his face like awnings over a café. If he isn't the murderer, why is he even on the show?

I watched the 2013 film version of *A Teacher*, written and directed by Hannah Fidell, her first indie feature. She is also the writer-director of the ten-episode FX series of the same name—both about female teachers having secret affairs with one of their male high school students. The film moves fast between moments in the woman's sexual obsession. She's already in the affair when the movie starts, and the movie ends when she knows her life is about to be ruined. It's a close-up on erotic thralldom. The boy offers little beyond his willingness to have sex and is baffled by the woman's responses to him. We can't care about their connection.

In the TV version, there is a considerable buildup to the relationship, and it makes sense to both of them. These two seem matched, however inconvenient and against current social norms their relationship is. No one is coerced, and no one is harmed inside the relationship. At the end of episode five, this teacher, too, is about to be ruined, and it isn't clear what we're supposed to make of anything we're shown. Disclaimers at the beginning and end of each episode alert young people to watch out for predators in the process of grooming them for unwanted sex—or, perhaps, for sex they do want and are told is bad for them.

What is churning in Fidell? I think it's the picture of a woman so erotically engaged that nothing else measures up and nothing else matters, including her own protection. We're not shown this very often from inside the consciousness of the woman, and for a little while on the show, these feelings aren't filed under *pathology*.

HUDSON, New York, December 4, 2020

Election night, when it looked like Biden might lose, I could not think of a reason to leave the couch—or remain on it. I was awake until 3:30. The next morning, I got out of bed after a woman texted to say she was coming to pick up chairs we were selling.

Back when I walked on Broadway, I would see a man with flowing white hair I had known in the past. He walked as much as I did and lived nearby. He was often singing to himself and seemed oblivious of me or others whizzing by, and although I did not stop to say hello, I would recall the excitement of the time when I'd met him in 1966 and I was nineteen. He had curly dark hair and worked for a trade newspaper that reported on scrap metal. He wrote all the pieces in the paper with headlines such as "Steel Prices Stainless" and "Nonferrous Market Resists Rust." The man I was married to was in law school and, as a part-time job, did market research at the scrap-metal paper. People liked him, and although the research he produced was pretty much fabricated, he was kept on and in time was able to hire me to help make things up.

The full-time writer was older than us and really a musician and songwriter. On weekends, he performed in a cabaret, and the man I was married to and I would go see him playing the piano and singing songs of soft satire. Lily Tomlin was performing there regularly, too, developing the characters she would soon present on *Laugh-In*. The writer was carefree, and I was grateful to be swept into a world I found glamorous and grown-up. He would hold little gatherings in his Hell's Kitchen walk-up. Actor friends would lean against exposed brick walls, holding juice glasses of wine. He wrote movie reviews for the newspaper, and when he went on vacation, I filled in for him. The reviews I wrote were my first published pieces. I would have followed anyone into a theater and wherever it led.

Some people are waiting for the pandemic to pass over like a weather condition. I like living in an airport lounge.

Recently, we watched *Reversal of Fortune* (1990) about Claus Von Bulow, who was acquitted of injecting his rich wife, Sunny, with enough insulin to place her in a permanent coma. The role requires Jeremy Irons to wear a partly bald prosthetic and look ghoulishly pale as he floats around in his imperious and clueless rich-man's way. The film makes you think about the tragic interior design choices of the ultrarich and how money buys freedom from accountability. It contrasts Claus's idle drifts from point A to point B to the dervish efforts of his lawyer, Alan Dershowitz, who, with his team of students and the aid of maids, hospital workers, bankers, lawyers, and the police, clean up the damage left behind by the moneyed class.

But whom would you rather have lunch with: Claus or Alan? Claus any day. Witty, self-deprecating Claus, unaware of his inappropriateness because he doesn't need to see it. The screenplay, based on the book by Dershowitz, advertises Dershowitz as the people's lawyer, fighting for the underdog and the right of anyone to have a strong defense, but you don't think that's who he is. He wants to win a splashy case because, as much as Claus wants to fade into the beige drapes, Dershowitz wants the limelight.

I used to practice tap steps waiting for trains. Everyone danced in the subway. The acoustics were good. I used to run to my sister at the flagpole at camp. She'd be twisting her ponytail and smelling of suntan oil. It's sexy to cut someone's hair. When I was a bartender, I was generous with the alcohol. I wanted people to be happy. For years in the 1960s and 1970s, I read Virago and Penguin editions of books by women: Virginia Woolf, Doris Lessing, and Colette in a gulp, the Margarets (Drabble and Atwood), Violette LeDuc, Jean Rhys, Gayl Jones, Sylvia Plath, Anne Sexton.

Before the pandemic, a friend invited me to a party. It was the renewal of a friendship that had come undone for reasons neither of us could understand. By this time, we had no idea who the other person had become. Still, warmth rose, and I forgot to eat. When I was young, I would see women from my future in the sauna. When you wonder if you should hide, it's because you forget you are always being seen.

Where I live now—on a farm road upstate—there are tall evergreens and field mice going nuts in the prickly winter grass. I wanted to offer them to the small owl discovered in the Christmas tree brought to Rockefeller Center. I have always wanted an owl. (Who hasn't?) Florence Nightingale rescued an owl in Greece she named Athena and took home with her to England. If the small Christmas tree owl came to live here, I wouldn't think it was mine. I would love it the way I love animals that aren't human—without judgment. In pictures, you can see the owl is thinking it's like accidentally stowing away on a plane and finding yourself in South America, where you have to learn another language it turns out you have an aptitude for, and it makes you think traveling reveals new parts of yourself as much as it reveals the world. You think about where your wings can take you, and you remember you are adorable to people. Humans think you look smarter than they look. The thing about a human is the hands that can lift you. Their hands are the future.

Last week, our sump pump died during twelve hours of rain. The battery died as well, and the apparatus was screaming as we waited for a plumber. At one point, the water in the well rose nearly to the basement floor, and the man I live with and I had to bail it out with buckets. He kept saying we would not be able to contain it, although it was clear if we kept going, we would. I filled the buckets, and he climbed the stone stairs to dump them outside. We got into a rhythm. He was carrying two buckets at a time. Fill, carry, hurl, and soon the level subsided. I knew absolutely we would not fail because no matter what, we would not stop. The man I live with knew absolutely we would not fail, but his way of knowing was to state the opposite.

On the phone the other day, a friend recalled the time she gave the man she was involved with a case of crabs. It was forty years ago. They had been in Denmark. He was an artist, preparing a show. She'd grown bored and returned to the States, where she'd slept with this one

— 77 —

and that one, the way we did. "It was a horrible thing to have done, so embarrassing, careless, and cruel," she said. And a few days later, when I spoke to her, I could see her self-judgment had increased. How could she have done such a thing to someone as kind and loving as this man?

I said, "Giving a person crabs because you had sex with other people doesn't sound that bad to me." Their affair was winding down, and what she'd done was her way out—cowardly, sure, but to me, ordinary. I said, "I have done many worse things." She said, "Like what?" I said I didn't feel like recalling the times I had been a heart-less betrayer, as examples flipped in my mind like a deck of cards. I thought that if giving a tender and trusting man a case of crabs was the worst thing you could see looking back, I could not imagine such a life. By any standard, my friend was a more honest and generous person than I'd ever been, and I was amazed she could stomach me.

I am thinking of the stripe of hipster that finds com-pliance with government authority uncool—a stripe that ironically or maybe not so ironically lines up with Trump defiers of masking and social distancing. And I wonder if it's thought less uncool to follow orders for the sake of others than to follow orders to save yourself. After the vaccine, will TV shows that resume production pretend COVID never happened? The man I live with says he will return to England if I die. This has given me a reason to live.

I have been thinking about the experience of re-experiencing a movie or book, and the way it makes you feel about your life. I remember seeing the films of Jean-Luc Godard as each came out, year after year, and loving them, especially *Pierrot le Fou* (1965) and *Weekend* (1967). Godard was the kind of person you were supposed to love, and I did love him. I think it was real love in the past.

It's not as if I've fallen out of love with his films. To fall out of love, you need the wear and tear of daily life, or the sudden awareness you have been living in a place where you do not know the language and have been wrong about the words. This once happened to me when I was visiting Germany. I thought I understood German because the German words sounded like Yiddish and because I started to walk and dream with the music of German in my head. I could taste the meaning of the words in the crusty bread from the bakery.

Last night, on Godard's birthday, we watched *Breathless* (1960). I don't remember the last time I saw it, but I remember the first time. Not what I thought about the movie. I remember who I was. Where could I have seen it? The Bleecker Street Cinema, probably. I remember the little jerseys with horizontal stripes worn by Jean Seberg. I wanted to wear a top like that. I thought Jean-Paul Belmondo was beautiful. I don't know what I thought, really, but the film, with its energy and jump cuts and, a couple of times, direct address to the viewer, and the music and sense of Paris and being a woman alone—a girl/woman on her own—this appealed to me when I was a girl/woman myself. I think, more than anything, seeing Seberg on the street with her not-even-trying, awful French accent called to me because she lived in a hotel.

Seeing the movie now, I didn't remember any of it as it actually is. I didn't remember that Belmondo pursues Seberg and she's not sure about him, which he likes, although he pretends not to. Somehow, you think she understands that if she acted like she was falling for him, she'd never see him again. I didn't remember the idiocy of their conversations that hover on the edge of boredom, the way the whole movie does. There is already a kind of boredom about life in these people and in the man who filmed them. Godard's camera loves each of them more than they feel for each other. They aren't sexy together. No heat rises off them. They kiss fake. They are two pretty birds on adjoining perches, fluffing out their feathers and pecking a bit on the other's wings before hopping off in another direction.

I didn't remember that Seberg shops him to the police or that everyone finds Belmondo's character, Michel, insufferable, while he doesn't see it. He's petulant, pushy, oblivious of Seberg's wishes or those of anyone else. The way the film thinks about women and understands women has nothing—really, nothing whatever—to do with how female people feel or understand the world and the ways they are perceived in it. The job of a woman in the world Godard depicts is to pretend not to see the contempt in which women are held. It's a full-time job. It's sometimes all any woman has time to do to get through life. I didn't care about Godard's infatuation with movies as he made a different kind of movie, although there is something to love about that. I'm just not the person to love it.

While I was watching, I wasn't bored as I balanced on the verge of boredom, like the characters. I could see Godard had made a piece of jazz from nothing and smoke. It was also like returning to the apartment building where I had lived as a young child to see how tiny the courtyard was. It was like returning to the summer camp where I had spent the happiest times of my childhood to find it abandoned and all the buildings leaning at an angle. Godard and the others in the

New Wave were inventing a new language of film, using all the old bones and props of ordinary understandings of what a man is and what a woman is.

The Christmas cactus in the bay window has bloomed. It isn't really a cactus. It isn't possible to will yourself to love anything. We love our new sheets that are gunmetal gray. I resist the social urging to feel doom. I was once at a decrepit artist residency so bleak and dirty I spent my days in the lobby of a nearby hotel, wearing headphones and using the Wi-Fi. At night, I watched *The Wire*, unable to stop looking at the pain of children, trapped in the drug world the show depicts. I kept borrowing the DVDs from the local library. When we bought the house where we live, I didn't understand what was needed to make it work. It was like falling in love—which is more or less resistance to feeling doom.

At the artist colony, I found funny the gap between feeling lucky to be there and feeling disgust at what it was. At another colony, I lived amid an infestation of stinkbugs no one tried to contain. In order to work or sleep, I vacuumed up hundreds of bugs from the furniture and walls several times a day. The thing about colonies is they are mostly uncomfortable in one way or another. You need to bring your own gunmetal gray sheets.

I wake up early in order to live longer. The sense I will never be done with anything or feel a sense of completeness helps me breathe. When I was twenty-five, I borrowed money from a friend to pay my rent and left behind as collateral a gold bracelet. People around Andy Warhol wondered if they should be more damaged or more whole.

A man came to fix the filtration system in our house and showed me videos of himself in the Grand Canyon. He was riding a mule in snow along the narrow path that cuts back and forth like a ribbon in the wind. I once visited the Grand Canyon at sunset. The rocks were on fire, and the man I had come with said, "It looks like the last day this is ever going to happen." In the videos the filtration man showed me, the air was gray above the icy Colorado River, and snow speckled the brown mules. The descent into the Canyon takes six hours and the climb back up takes eight hours along a mile of stairs.

In the Before, one night, I was walking in Manhattan with the man who had taken me to the Grand Canyon when I tripped on the sidewalk outside a Rite Aid. This man was now my former boyfriend, and my lip was bleeding. The store had the blue-gray air of a space station. People were poring over heart-shaped boxes of chocolates and violent computer games, pretending not to notice the blood dripping from my lip. A young man with a thin mustache led my ex-boyfriend and me to the employees' toilet down a hallway lined with soft drinks and scouring cleansers. My former boyfriend had dark, flowing hair. I had bitten my lip in two places, and the inside was visible, like a palm turning out. He said, "You won't be the worst-looking person on the subway." He was wrong. Before he left, I said, "I want to hold your hand." He took my hand, sticky with blood, and kissed it. In time, a small scar formed on my lip.

All the trees have dropped their leaves, and the branches are jumping in the wind. For women, the past has no information. In 1968, the house of famous modernist and anti-Semite Louis-Ferdinand Céline burned down, destroying manuscripts, furniture, and mementos. His parrot, Toto, remained safe in an adjacent aviary. In the 1990s, I found myself friends with a number of people who'd been junkies. By the time I was born, there was a television in the house. I watched it from a couch splashed with red dahlias. To eat clams from the shell, my father would throw back his head and smile. As the youngest child, I didn't imagine living an adult life. I could have taken the same fall at twenty.

HUDSON, New York, February 2021

The man I live with digs out snow so our solar unit can follow the sun. There is no sun. Where are the birds? The other day, I laid decorative tiles beneath the serial killer's furnace in our basement and accidentally produced a design in the shape of a swastika.

We didn't buy the house from an actual serial killer (maybe). The rusty freezer for storing body parts, the clothes piled amid spider webs, the ceiling hooks and metal chains coiled on the basement floor and suspended from the stained walls, were so specific. You don't hear enough Scriabin on the radio. When I fluff my hair for Zoom, I reach for perfume. Then I think: schmendrick, that was a different life.

The great grief at the heart of *The Wizard of Oz* (1939) is that the wish to return to a black-and-white world is a lie. Auntie Em, who hands over Dorothy's dog to a woman of power and influence in the town, is not a person anyone would want to see again, and you catch this in the strained expression on Judy's face as she clicks the heels of her ruby slippers. Also, there's no song in the movie about *returning* from the rainbow.

We are watching *Call My Agent!*, the French TV series streaming on Netflix, and so far, it's *please don't let it end, please keep us so we won't be left adrift again in the tragic suggestions of other people.* In season two, Andréa, who is gay, winds up having angry, hot sex with a man she detests and who has bought the talent agency where she's a partner. His acquisition is owing to her, and it's something she quickly regrets, and also has to accommodate in that without him, the company will go under.

Their paths have crossed at an award ceremony back in her hometown, where they are both being celebrated for doing well enough to leave the backwater. She feels distaste from the moment she lays eyes on him, with his man bun and teasing, angry manner with her, using a name she has changed, on and on. He wants to break her, in that it's his way of moving in the world.

In one scene, he asks her to change into a dress he has bought her to seduce a client he wants to steal from another agency. She refuses to change into the dress in front of him, making clear the limits of her compliance. But another night, they are both drunk and both making out with a beautiful model in a hotel room, when suddenly they go at it with each other, abandoning the woman who says, "Hey, over here" (in French) before slipping off. We watch the former outcasts take each other's faces in their hands and tear each other to pieces.

The scene made me happy in its tender acceptance of sexual weirdness and the great comic truth that desire is larger than what we can know. Once, at a party, a man I secretly wanted to touch came over and kissed me. I didn't push him away. His hands were on my shoulders. His tongue was in my mouth. It was a good kiss, as if we'd been doing it for a while. After my father died, my mother wasn't that old, and I remember walking on a beach with her as she looked around for her life. I pulled away from the man who kissed me and said, "You're acting like a lunatic." I didn't really say that. I said, "I love you" (in French).

For several weeks, I used prison-grade toilet paper that was free. I had to use it until it was finished, the way some people tap on a wall five times before they can leave a room. On two separate occasions, the market where we shop sent me a coupon for two free packages of prison-grade toilet paper, and I took the toilet paper because it would not have been possible for me not to. In my twenties, I was seeing a shrink, and one Christmas, I knitted him a pair of mittens. The following Christmas, I knitted him another pair of mittens with the exact same wool. When he asked me the significance of the repeated gift, I saw my interest in what we were doing was fake.

We watched a Danish show on HBO called *The Investigation*. The chief of police is telling the parents of a journalist their daughter may be dead, and everyone looks like a monument on Mount Rushmore—no expression you can read, and no voices raised. I said to the man I live with, "Imagine this scene with Italians." Then I said, "I should become more Danish." He said, "It would help."

An orange has been engineered so it's easy to peel. It's the ones that are hard to peel that hold our attention. I once answered an ad on Craigslist to visit the home of a stranger who was giving away tea. Not only tea, but the accoutrements of tea making, including kettles and pottery. He was in the business and had too much in his house, owing to circumstances I don't need to tell you. He inhabited an entire brownstone in the West Village, and I was excited by the proximity of my abjection to luxury. He opened the door and led me to the parlor floor, where cartons were waiting. I couldn't carry all the things I wanted and would have given to people I knew could use them. He was slight and looked weary. He said he had a cold and curled up on the couch. I was on the floor with the boxes. He said, "Are you dangerous?" I needed to give him something. I said, "Yes."

A week ago I posted an image on Facebook of two baby owls. Two puffballs, their twig toes wrapped around a branch, with tiny triangular beaks and pin-point eyes behind which it was easy to imagine wit and joy. Within seconds, the image prompted excited reactions—forty or fifty shares and shares of shares. Nothing I had posted before drew such a response, and I quickly resented the owls. On closer inspection, their beaks are mysterious. You don't know if the small triangle is supposed to represent a nose or a mouth. They look as though they don't have mouths, and I was reminded of the body artists David Wojnarowicz and Petr Pavlensky, who sewed together their lips as a form of protest. There is no telling where a chain of associations is going to wind up.

The man I live with is concerned for the plight of bur-glars, who, these days, cannot schedule break-ins, since everyone is home. He's alert as well to the struggle of robbers at gas stations and convenience stores, who have become indistinguishable from everyone else wearing a mask. How can you be certain this is the right person to empty your cash register for?

The other day, I got into a conversation on Facebook about what was meant by the term *radical feminism* in 1967, when I joined the women's movement. I said we meant what Shulamith Firestone meant by feminism: a fundamental rethinking of sex and gender categories and the effects of that rethinking on society. It was all up for grabs, and someone on the comment thread asked if that much had changed for women as a result of all the rethinking, and I said evenly—because I didn't want to act like the dick I am—that everything had changed, and the example I gave was that white, monied, heterosexual men didn't used to be a category.

I started thinking about the thinking that underlies such a question, the way people don't want to see what's altered because everything hasn't altered, and what came to mind was a joke Leonard Michaels tells in his essay, "My Yiddish." According to Michaels, the joke expresses the incongruity and forbearance that are quintessentially loaded into the Yiddish language and Jewish humor, and I'm going to tell you the joke and say something after.

"*The rabbi says, 'What's green, hangs on the wall, and whistles?'*
The student says, 'I don't know.'
The rabbi says, 'A herring.'
The student says, 'Maybe a herring could be green and hang on a wall, but it absolutely doesn't whistle.'
The rabbi says, 'So it doesn't whistle.'"

What I want to say to the person who asked if anything for women had changed after fifty years of feminists *hocking* everyone to death, day and night, about sexism and misogyny is: so we didn't fix everything.

I decided to stop drinking and to walk on the road every day. I have resumed drinking and have not been outside for four days. I was sad without alcohol, and the house had too few rooms. Last night, a box was delivered by our neighbor, who owns a liquor store in a town some miles away. Drinking is a new constant for me. Change is good.

I mixed a pitcher of COVID cocktails, and the man I live with ruffled my hair. It was in need of a cut. I thought maybe I should get a cat instead of a cut. I asked him if he was up for telly this early. It was only five o'clock. We tried an Israeli show called *Losing*

Alice, in which all the women are beautiful and sexy and all the men—really *all* the men—are dentists and accountants from central casting—even the husband, who is often half-naked. Within the yawning range of female appetite, these men do not cut it. A great Israeli hoax is being perpetrated.

Yesterday, I was reading *The Paris Review* and came upon an appreciation of *Shadow of a Doubt* (1943), the Hitchcock movie starring Teresa Wright and Joseph Cotten, who plays her uncle and turns out to be a serial murderer. Suddenly, I remembered I'd *known* Teresa Wright in her later years, and we'd met a few times at Popover Café on Amsterdam Avenue. I remember sitting across from her and seeing the young face in the old one.

We first met in 1990 after a performance she gave at Berkshire Theatre Festival in Athol Fugard's play *The Road to Mecca*. The reason I remember any of it is I wrote about the production when I wrote about the death of the man I was with at the time. The play is about an aging artist who is nearly destroyed by isolation and is yet sustained by her work, and that man, whose name was Gardner, and I had sat weeping through the evening. It was August of 1990, and by December 17, he would be dead. Teresa came out to talk to us after the rest of the audience had left, maybe because I was a reviewer for *The Village Voice*. Maybe that's why she met with me afterward in New York.

I'm straining to recall a single thing we talked about. Did she tell me about her daughter? Her career in Hollywood? I was interested that she still wanted to act. She was seventy-two, younger than I am now. During the play, she was onstage for the entire two hours, and at one point delivered a monologue that runs for four pages. At the time of Gardner's death and my meetings with her, I was forty-three, and when you are forty-three and talking to a person in their seventies, they seem to occupy a different plane of existence. This is something I cannot keep in mind now, that when I interact with people several decades younger than me, they are probably seeing an exhibit on a plinth.

I was always interested in pushing myself against people with fame. Teresa Wright was so real, the element of her fame was quickly absorbed into the tender and sincere way she looked at me and asked about my life. I think we met after Gardner's death. The memory is sweet. She was soft as a petal and generous. I remember nothing, really, except that it happened.

A few nights ago, I couldn't sleep, thinking about the everything and nothing of late night. It reminded me of my old life in my apartment, in the quiet and expansiveness of solitude. I used to let my dog off the leash in Riverside Park, and when he would wander too far for me to see him and I would be shouting for him like a lunatic, I felt like I was going to die of grief, and I thought the dog was me in his indifference to control.

I miss sex with strangers—not the sex itself but the possibility of something happening. I don't believe in the concept of *wisdom*. It isn't a real thing. It's the bone the young toss to the old when they are going into your life to rob you of your sense of self. The moon is making the snow outside bright enough for shadows. I'm happy talking to you.

HUDSON, New York, March 2021

I have been following the dispatches of Italian novelist Francesco Pacifico, writing about COVID from Rome for *n+1*, and I have fallen in love with the way his mind works on the page. We get to feel him and know him, smell him, almost taste him—he is that intimate. Not confessional, not really. It's a trick of language and the way it can seduce the reader into a proximity that's only in their heads.

The majority of the latest dispatch is a thought experiment about wanting to peel off the advantages Pacifico feels he has as a man and, as the editor of a magazine, open the pages to women writers. It means rejecting the writing of lots of younger male writers who take a particular stand in life because they are men. Pacifico describes the stand in a satirical passage I couldn't hold in my head because I don't care about these men. He hates them and is happy to reject them. He hates men in general, and here, of course, he is a sympathetic narrator.

He doesn't really hate men. He doesn't really hate himself, and he doesn't really know what's bugging him about the sense of social and economic power he believes he was born with and that he doesn't really want to surrender. Not one jot of it, he admits, and you think, What are you talking about? And should you be talking out loud?

In the '70s, I remember it was a thing for some men who were struck on the head by the fallen brick of sexual politics and the sudden awareness that sexism and misogyny guided all human relations. They were so upset and unhappy being on the team that gains from the unfairness, they called themselves *feminines* or something like that. I didn't look it up. It was a thing. It didn't last, thank god. They weren't trying to be what is now called trans. I only bring it up to say Pacifico's sense of discomfort has a historical basis.

Not only is it not new, it has nothing to do with women or helping women or being less sexist. It's just a thing some men go through. And the way you know it has nothing to do with women is Pacifico doesn't have a concrete thing to say about the writing of the women he invites into the magazine. He says it changed him. He says he preferred reading them to men. But what did they say that was different from their male peers? Is it a stylistic thing they are inventing that is distinct? He doesn't specify a single piece that changed him, made him feel something he'd not felt before. He isn't looking at them. The fact of them is instrumental to his sense of struggle-as-a-man—at least, as far as the piece he is writing is concerned.

The dispatch is like a big fat any-love-song by Bob Dylan, in which the singer nags the woman and proclaims his desire and need and being driven out of his mind by her but does not depict *her*. What color are her eyes? What does she look like when she isn't paying attention to him, when she's with her female friends and he watches from another room? (By the way, every fight I've ever had with the man I live with is basically about Bob Dylan.)

Instead of looking at women (even the one female editor at the magazine he plots with isn't visible to us), Pacifico includes in the dispatch a series of notes written by his editor as the piece was developing, and this editor, who is a man, doesn't mention the thing I just mentioned about describing the writing of the women Pacifico solicits and why it matters to him. The editor points out various sorts of contradictions that are actually interesting and from which there is no way out, and points out Pacifico may be gleeful about rejecting males in order to be king of the heap.

What the editor means is only the writing of other men constitutes the heap.

They like talking about power and what power means to each of them. This kind of power and that kind of power. And what you feel as you read the piece is that it's actually a series of love letters between the men in the form of a sparring match, to see who can think better, and they both love it. They are really into it, and you feel their enjoyment—it's the most alive aspect of the piece—and you think, Fine, great. But if you are me, you think, This has nothing to do with me. Being powerful in the world of letters in the terms these men consider—none of it is the way I understand my experience as a writer.

HUDSON, New York, July 2021

I bought five ears of corn for a friend who was coming to visit. She said her front teeth were temporary and she might need to cut the kernels off the cob. It rained, and the grilling was canceled. When I opened the fridge today, I saw a canvas bag in the bottom bin. Inside the bag were five different ears of corn. From a month ago? A year ago? There was mold and blackened bits but no smell—five decomposing little corpses, each wrapped in its own shroud. Was this my house?

I remember stepping off the bus from the airport in Newark and wheeling my bag through Times Square. I would look out the window of the uptown bus, recalling every shop and patch of green along the route, until I was on my street and home, in a manner of speaking. I never liked where I lived, not really. It was a marriage of convenience. When you live in New York City, you love most that you live in New York City.

The man I live with told me he imagined living on after me. He does this from time to time, as I do with him, except I don't see my life without him. Everything slips from my mind. I said, "Don't kill me off, even in your imagination." He said if I died, he would sell our house.

Last night, I was staying with a friend in Massachusetts. I woke up and thought I might not be peeing enough, and so I got up and peed. The man I live with said he also imagines me living on after him. I said to my friend, "I wouldn't sell our house." She looked past me and said, "You don't know what you'd do." When was the last time I surprised myself? I think it was the other day, when I realized I misread people more often than I understand what was going on between us. Once a thought like this forms, it seeps over your entire life like the orange drops used to numb your corneas during an eye exam.

This month, during our sessions of streaming, the man I live with and I watched two movies emblematic of their times and two current TV series.

One of the old movies was *A League of Their Own* (1992). The man I live with was all like, "Tom Hanks, you are such a bad actor, you can't even play a drunk." I liked the movie's sentimental version of feminism, where you look at a forgotten phenomenon, like women in baseball during World War II, and show how women—with economic backing and more control over their lives than in domesticity—wake up to the power of their bodies. Madonna is adorable with partner Rosie O'Donnell when they were besties IRL too. Madonna isn't allowed to take over the film by director Penny Marshall, and Madonna looks like she's having a very good time, diving face first into home base and dancing with strangers in a bar.

The movie belongs to Geena Davis and to the ambivalence her character feels about claiming her own life. She can't do it, ultimately, and the film shows us the social reasons why. As the credits roll, we see the real players from the league, now aged, playing a game, and they are wonderful—still walking with butch swagger, still tearing around the bases in a way they might not be able to run for a bus. Movies about female athletes are always thrilling. The body lifts off from the ways it is understood and falls in love with defying gravity.

The other old movie was *Rosemary's Baby*. I saw it when it was released in 1968, a second time I don't remember, and a third time last week. In 1966, when I was nineteen, I married a boy I don't exactly know why. I loved him, but married? I mean, I don't know what I mean. The day I got married, I knew I shouldn't do it.

In 1968, I noticed that in the movie Mia Farrow is dressed in the clothes of a child or a puppet—pinafores and Peter Pan collars. She is the yellow of a sunflower, and her apartment in the gray Dakota is also yellow. I don't remember if, in 1968, I registered that her husband laughs off raping her while she's asleep and that it turned him on. She looks more confused than angry. She isn't allowed to show anger in the world she lives in until she realizes her husband pimped her to the devil for better acting parts.

There's so much pleasure in this film. It stays with you days later, like Rosemary's sense that sex with the devil was real and not a dream. Much of the film's brilliance is in the casting. Ruth Gordon's performance as Minnie Castevet is genius in the details: the way she twists the fork in her mouth while eating cake, the way she sniffs out the price tags on the things in Rosemary's apartment. As soon as we see the smirk on the mouth of John Cassavetes—it's permanent, it's the way he looks at life—we know that nothing that happens to Rosemary is as bad as having married him. Whether or not Roman Polanski consciously set out to do this, he made a movie in which the deep, dark horror is ordinary bourgeois marriage.

Of course Rosemary will rock the devil she has given birth to. How much worse can a devil be than her husband and the other humans who have used her? Satan, by comparison, is bland and *meh*, like the members of the coven, composed of social strays shunned not for their demonic powers but their social awkwardness. In any movie with Charles Grodin, he is going to be a snake. The movie is a comedy. It's why we don't need to see the demon baby.

The trees leafed up earlier this year than last, I think. People are writing to me in dreams who don't write to me in real life. A friend wrote to say he'd grown depressed after the people who were staying in his house during the pandemic went back to their lives. Did they think they were returning to who they'd been before? In Long Beach, the rain falls sideways during hurricanes. If you step into it, it feels like nails flying at you, and it is intensely pleasurable.

When I read remarks prefaced with a series of identity markers like a bar code—as a gay, het, trans, white, Black, disabled, poor, rich, and so on—as if this is who you are, I think: This is not who you are. I think who you are is the tomato you grew and served to a friend. I think: You are your face in sleep. You are the way you lick the bowl and hold out your hand for a dog to sniff.

I hate-watched season four of *The Handmaid's Tale* so you don't have to. The chief appeal of this show has always been Elisabeth Moss doing anything—staring into space with the tips of her front teeth peeking from the curtain of her lips, testing the sharpness of a knife before a murder of revenge, whispering escape plans in the ear of a young woman whose eye has been gouged out for some damn infraction in Gilead. The powers in Gilead believe in God and the sanctity of motherhood; that's what justifies the wrongs of their society. In Canada, opponents of Gilead *also* believe in God and the sanctity of motherhood! That's what's wrong with the show. It's an advertisement for religion in both directions. The heart-tugging music. The pieties flying from everyone's lips. In one bit of dialogue so demented you can see it hurting the underutilized Samira Wiley, her character chides Moss for not thinking ahead when she rescued eighty-nine children from a murderous theocracy and packing some Gilead memorabilia for when they got homesick. Like a pillow embroidered with the phrase "under his eye"?

Hacks on HBO—about a stand-up comedian—is enjoyable to watch, mainly owing to the rapport of leads Jean Smart and Hannah Einbinder. The most startling sequence occurs in episode eight, the finale, when Smart's character goes to a small comedy club to try out new material and the male MC introduces her with a series of insults. Smart's character, who is famous and rich, offers to pay him 1.7 million dollars if he agrees never to set foot on a stage again, adding that if he accepts the deal and afterward performs, he will owe her double that amount. He accepts the offer, of course, because his comedy no longer matters, the crowd affirms, egging him to take the money and disappear.

This scene follows one in which Smart and a female crony from her touring years recall the club owners who groped them and the slams from male comics they smiled through. The friends are meant to be in their sixties. The young woman they are with, who is in her twenties, is upset the older women felt they had no choice but to go along. She wants to nudge them into a #MeToo moment without blaming them, although she does blame them. Smart takes in what the young woman says. It prompts her handling of the MC.

The problem with the incident and with the show as a whole is chronology. It's as if only twentysomethings get feminism and seem to have invented it. Smart plays a kind of Joan Rivers comic, who sells things on QVC and sells out her intelligence in her act. If Joan Rivers were alive, she would be eighty-eight. Joan was young enough to have become a feminist in the 1960s and 1970s and to have changed her shtick, but she didn't. It doesn't matter.

Smart's character was in her teens and early twenties when the women's movement shook the planet-- whether in excited agreement or raging opposition. A woman the age of Smart's character would not need to hear about any of this from a twentysomething. She would have heard it from the movement, even if she was outside it. Smart's character says to the younger woman, who is helping her write a new show, "Yes, yes, I know, I know, but how to make it funny?" That is always the question.

A visitor came today, and when we hugged, our faces touched. The visitor reminded me of people in general. It was like remembering I used to know how to juggle. I had a boyfriend once who was a cheater. I wasn't with him long enough to lose interest in him. That was his gift to me.

Recently, I had a bout of excellent sleep. It was scary. I wondered if something was wrong. One bird chirps the same three notes: "pretty, pretty, pretty." Other birds are talking about trains. It's about to rain. There is dirt under my nails. The peonies are up to my knees.

HUDSON, New York, August 2021

The thing about limits is there's something to be said for them. Take you and me: When I was young, I would have had sex with you, and it would have been good. I would have thought it was good because I was into the look of you. I would have thought the sex was good because of how happy it made me to be with you on the top of a mountain. Not on grass—I never liked grass for sex, or sand. For the sex to be good, I thought it meant what had happened inside me had also happened inside you. Until last week, I didn't see, not really, this isn't true at all as a principle, although it could also be the case that the sex I thought was good between me and another person had made the other person happy, too.

We would have met at a party or at an event where there was free food and free drinks, and I would have slipped beside you and said something with a smile. During a certain period, we would have had sex in my apartment. I wouldn't have been afraid to bring you back there. I would think from the way we were talking that I had nothing to fear. Fear wasn't that much a part of things at that time. I would have rested my head in the crook of your arm and thought I should relax.

After you got up from the bed, you might have given me a small thought as you were getting dressed or hailing a cab and lighting up a smoke. I would never see you again, and I would remember you for the rest of my life. I would remember you because of the space between what had happened to me and what had happened to you.

I would remember you because it would flash clearly for a moment that I had been so wrong it was funny, and then I would forget it so the same thing could happen with someone else. The thing about limits is this can no longer happen. I cannot fully express how happy it makes me to tell you this.

Yesterday, the man I live with and I bought two shelving units in the shape of ladders from a man in Chatham, New York. He was wearing a T-shirt that exposed his arms and chest and made him look like a character in a play by Arthur Miller. In those days, everyone had to write at least one play about inconvenient homosexuality. The man was friendly and alive as he unscrewed the units from the wall. There was a mezuzah on his door. He was telling us a story about

Jews and the travels of Jews around the world. There were too many details, and I broke in and said, "You know you're talking to a Jew?" His head moved back the tiniest bit, and he sped up the story. Only in Chatham would someone not take me for a Jew. Even a Jew.

We watched *Klute* (1971) as part of our adventures in rewatching old movies. The film is named after the male detective played by Donald Sutherland. It should have been named *Shag*, after Jane Fonda's haircut, or *Maxiskirt*, which, in reality, no one in the 1970s wore for more than five minutes because they were so ugly. Not even Jane can make them work. In reality, too, we weren't all named after a cheese (Jane's name here is Bree) and we didn't speak to our johns with boarding-school diction. Donald's diction is crisp as well. It's a pleasure to hear them enunciate all their syllables.

I liked the pacing of the movie. The way the story is told in scene chunks that don't connect all the dots, the way there is no backstory, just the *now* of events. I loved Jane's sessions with her smart female shrink. Jane is seeing a shrink because every time she passes a phone booth (a phone booth!!!), she calls her connection to arrange a trick. Jane's monologues about what she likes about prostitution amount to: "I want to feel in control of something." We see her turned down again and again for acting and modeling jobs. In the sessions with the shrink, she says the same thing about wanting control. It was a new insight then, and in these scenes we feel the women's movement breathing on the screen.

I enjoyed watching the love story unfold between Jane and Donald. Jane is on-screen in almost every shot, and she's adorable with her sadness and the beautiful mouth of her distant dad. Alan Pakula directed it, and you can see the male human straining to hear something of the moment he's living in, although in the end the girl at the center is still a prostitute. That's the thing she will look back on in her life and think, Wow, I did something scary and on my own terms, and I was really good at telling men what they wanted to hear. And so, angel/whore remains the only deal in town. And still, Jane must stupidly set herself up for a great risk in order to be rescued by a man. That's not something that would happen in a movie now with a female at the center.

We are in Maine, and I wanted a lobster. The man I live with and our host both said, "I don't want a lobster. They're too much trouble to eat." I said, "I like the trouble." I went to the pier near where our host lives and ordered a lobster to pick up at 6 p.m. I ordered a two-and-a-half-pound lobster, cooked.

Back at the house, our host said, "Where did you order the lobster?" When I told her, she said, "They're Trumpers and fervent antivaxxers. Did you wear a mask?" I said I did. I said, "I'll cancel the order and go to the co-op." It was where she said she shopped now. She said, "Don't cancel the order. It's only one lobster."

I have to tell you the woman who had waited on me at the counter was also named Laurie. She was very pretty—I could tell because no mask. We made small talk. This was before I knew about the Trump and antivaxxer thing. When I went to pick up the lobster, even knowing the politics of the place, I fell into the same easy banter with Laurie. We wished each other a pleasant evening. It didn't seem there was anything else to do.

There I was, with my warm lobster in a bag. I was hungry. I was also the designated cook. If you know me, you know why. Before I could eat the lobster, I made a meal for the man I live with and our host, and while they were eating, I removed the lobster from the bag and put the thing on a plate. The lobster had not been prepared for eating. I had a nutcracker and a pick, and we were outside on one of the decks that over-look a bay dotted with small boats and floating rafts, and the sea gulls were circling overhead, wondering when they would get a turn at the shells. I could see the feathers of their bellies, tinged pink by the setting sun.

My lobster did not weigh two and a half pounds. It was small, really, and cold and wet. As I worked on it, it exuded a sodden hopelessness, and a few times the rubbery mess squirted onto my pants and shirt and even my toes in my flip-flops. There is no moral to this story. There is no story to any moral. My lobstery clothes are rolled up in two balls, quarantined from the other clothes. They are the clothes of infamy. You can decide why.

A man I didn't know died, and there was a sale of his belongings. The man running the sale said the man had died of being old. The man running the sale was neither very old nor very young. By the time I arrived, the house was mobbed. You had to take a number, like at Zabar's, to get in. The house was a mansion on the main avenue of a small town upstate. Each of the many rooms was crammed with objects—it was an explosion.

The walls were lined with framed images arranged close together, like stamps in a book. There were multiples of linens and kitchenware and vases and pillows and things from Japan and China and Africa he just had to have. Everything the man had owned was for sale, even two garnet-colored terry robes that must once have been plush and now were a study in pulled threads. Had relatives and friends already sifted out what they wanted? I didn't think so. I thought, *This is the world he lived in and walked away from, as if stepping out to buy milk.*

I had come for things in the garden. I bought a tall pillar made of concrete that was very heavy. The man running the sale lifted it in his arms and set it in the back of my car. He cushioned it with the canvas bags I keep there for groceries. He said he knew the man who had died and called him by name. He said he had been in the house many times and didn't charge me for a sugar and creamer set engraved with the initials of someone else. Like me, the man who had died liked belongings from other people's lives. The man running the sale told me his name and patted the column in the back of my car. He said, "Goodbye." He said, "Don't brake fast."

I have been watching the Ronan Farrow tapes on HBO, where he markets his triumph in nailing Harvey Weinstein. What was the deal with Weinstein's repetition? It crossed my mind that, for him, while enacting a scenario of coercion with woman after woman, he gets to see their loathing. And this loathing must do something to him he needs to keep feeling. He knows

he is loathsome, and in each encounter this is con-
firmed, and it makes him sad, and in Harvey's case,
sadness leads to anger. And anger stirs aggression. In
me, too (you should excuse the expression), sadness
moves in a flash to anger, and anger is the bitter story
of my life.

In my early days in Scottsdale with the man I live with
now, we were strolling back from the communal
dumpster at the place where we lived when I spotted
a plastic pail in front of a hedge. Inside the pail was
what looked like a dead stick, and I said, "Let's take
it home." There was green under the stick's brown
husks, and in time, a shoot poked up and slowly
unfurled—it was a species of palm I recognized from
a park nearby. The park was not really a park but part
of the system of washes that collect water during the
brief but massive desert downpours. During the thirteen years we cared for the palm, it grew to be a tree
over eight feet tall. When we were packing to leave
Arizona for good, I asked our neighbor if she would
adopt it, and when she said she would, all concern
about the move fell away. This is the neighbor I would
call from New York when I couldn't get the man I live
with on the phone and knew he was having a low
blood sugar. She would find the hidden key and she
would find the man, often naked in bed. I would hear
her on the other end of the line saying, "Come on,

Richard, have some orange juice," as she propped him up and held a glass to his lips.

People on Facebook are asking white male filmmakers and white male writers for the hamburger with a salad on the side instead of the fries. The white males want to serve the hamburger, as always, with fries. These men have lived their lives believing everyone was interested in them when everyone was not interested in them. On our road is a farm with sheep, and each day, as we approach the farm, we wonder whether the sheep will be standing or sitting, whether they'll be inside their enclosure or wandering about their pens. I can't tell if I am recovering from the injury to my back at the same speed I would have recovered when I was younger, or if the injury is so horrendous I should be happy I can right myself like a turtle and scuttle off at all. Our lives in retrospect are stray cats.

Today I read we will never be rid of the virus, although it may grow less lethal. The Munchkin sequence in *The Wizard of Oz* goes on and on, and you can see Judy thinking, *Please, God, make it stop*. Rain is jumping over stones at the back of our house with the force of our beating hearts.

Elsewhere, Elsewhen

Seven Locations

LONDON, England June 1995

Last night, I walked from Piccadilly Circus past Green Park to Hyde Park, across Knightsbridge and Kensington, then north up a street of antique shops called Kensington Church Street to Notting Hill Gate, then across a winding road that led into Indian neighborhoods and to the M-4 highway, then Edgware Road, then across St John's Wood Road, then up Wellington to Finchley Road and back to West Hampstead, where I was staying. My friend said, "Are you thinking interesting thoughts on your walks? It seems to me you do nothing but move."

SOUTHAMPTON, Long Island, August 2002

I was in a van, waiting for waiters to arrive. My friend said, "I rescued a chicken that escaped from a slaughterhouse in my neighborhood." My friend was small and dark-haired. It was noon on a Saturday, and I was driving the van. My friend was from Uruguay and had named the chicken Pepita. She said, "She's following my cats around." I said, "Do you still eat chicken?" She said, "Yes, just not this one."

On the way to Southampton, I smelled ocean before it was visible. When we arrived at the venue, we were told the client didn't want us in her house for any reason. We were to use two small outdoor toilets and wash our hands in the garage. The champagne bottles were not to be discarded, so she could count them. We were not to take flowers, although more than a hundred arrangements of roses, peonies, tulips, Casa Blanca lilies, and delphiniums sat on twenty-five tables.

Three tents were pitched on the lawn. One housed the kitchen. Another was for the reception, furnished with couches, silk cushions, carpets, and tables. The third was the dining room, vaulting up like a circus big top and lit with Japanese lanterns.

I folded napkins into origami nests and cut baguettes into slivers. I lit votive candles and filled water glasses. My job at dinner was to replenish stations of French and Asian food. At nine o'clock, two hundred guests streamed into the dining tent, where waiters, poised with serving tongs, stood stationed before chaffing dishes and platters. There were short ribs the size of fists, braised black outside and buttery within. On another platter was a medley of baby vegetables, as well as morels and a puree of garlic potatoes. There were thick wedges of quiche, seafood ravioli, platters of fat, green-and-white asparagus with an egg lemon sauce, and two kinds of cold soup: carrot ginger and five pea, garnished with prosciutto lardons. The Asian table was laid with green papaya salad, Peking duck, sesame noodles, various stir-fries, pad thai, spring rolls, and steamed dumplings filled with chunks of lobster and shrimp. Dom Pérignon and Cristal flowed.

For two hours, the pace did not slow. The men wore loafers without socks. The women wore pointy stilettos that sank into the grass between the tents. After the main courses were cleared, the men smoked cigars, and we poured brandy. At eleven thirty, we served coffee and dessert, setting down individual warm chocolate soufflés, raspberry tarts filled with pastry cream, and chocolate mousse bombs shaped like plump mice with praline noses and curly chocolate tails. Each plate contained mini scoops of pistachio and passion fruit ice cream nestled in thin, ruffled cookies. Last, we served plates of petits fours and chocolate truffles.

I was about to leave the dining room to eat out of sight of the guests when I saw a man I knew and with whom in the past I'd had mean, secret sex. I turned in the smoky light to make sure it was really him. There he was, in a maroon jacket wrong for the season, talking over his shoulder to a man in light-colored slacks and a navy blazer. What was my former friend, the former Marxist, doing at the party of a woman who searched our bags for stolen things? What was I doing here? The man's hair was thinning, and he had developed a small paunch. I remembered him slender and naked. I had once bought him a shirt he wore until it became a rag. I didn't want him to see me in a tux, although for this to happen I would have had to thrust my face directly into his. Guests do not look at servers. If they had to pick you out of a lineup, you would beat the rap. The next time I swept the room, he was talking to a man with a ruddy complexion and pink slacks. I bumped my nose on the metal corner of a table. I used a bathroom designated for the guests. I ate a chocolate mouse. I couldn't keep stalling. He kept talking until the band stopped playing. Finally, he drifted into the night.

Nine men and I stayed for the final breakdown. By then, we had been on our feet and moving for seven hours. It started to rain. There were bars to break down, tubs of ice to cart and dump, bottles of liquor to wipe dry and box, hundreds of glasses to slop and place in lugs, hundreds of plates to scrape and crate, dozens of tables to fold, wheel, and stack, hundreds of chairs to bag and stack, dozens of cocktail tables to disassemble. Linens needed to be collected and bagged, kitchen equipment crated, and garbage hauled.

Our group included actors, dancers, and a photographer, all under thirty. I was fifty-four. The men came from Brazil, France, Spain, India, Afghanistan, and Greenwich, Connecticut. I knew where they had gone to school, who they were sending money to back home, who they were sleeping with. The tasks were messy. We called each other *sweetheart* and *darling*.

At two in the morning, we were done. Before starting the van, I popped an Advil and drank a Diet Coke for the caffeine. One of the Brazilians ruffled my hair and stretched out on the back seat. An actor sat up front with me, and we talked while the others slept. He worked as a security guard at an apartment complex, wandering the grounds that overlooked the Hudson and memorizing monologues.

The rain quit after a while, and I sped along. Some of the guys had jobs the next day and would get only a few hours' sleep. A couple tumbled out groggily in Queens. The rest peeled off in Manhattan. At five, I rolled into the garage to return the van and felt a second wind. I walked uptown as the sky turned milky, feeling unsettled in a way that was familiar and that I would never get used to.

GROUND ZERO, New York City, September 2001
A few days after the planes hit the Towers, I joined a group of volunteers at Ground Zero. A friend knew a young Anglican priest with a wealthy parish on the Upper East Side. The attacks of 9/11 gave her something gritty to do. She was English and beautiful, and with her accent and upbringing, she could be earnest and witty at the same time. As a priest delivering last rites over dead bodies and human remains, she had special access to the site.

We watched her say last words, wearing a white vestment and looking down at dusty rubble and torqued metal. After that, we were taken to Trinity Church and from there to Bouley Bakery to prepare meals for the workers at the site. I had never been to Bouley Bakery, but I knew how to work in a restaurant kitchen. I remember there was a long, stainless-steel table, where strudel dough was extruded from a machine. We did not make strudel.

We worked all night until the sun came up. Other days after that, I was able to return to prepare meals for the workers. My friend was a journalist. At the end of our long shift, we were giddy and wobbly, but not tired. We stood outside the fenced area of devastation and watched it change colors in the reddish glow of the rising sun. Workers in hard hats moved around, searching for things or nothing. There were vans from the Red Cross in the streets, dispensing the food we'd prepared. A certain kind of camaraderie forms around disasters, and all of New York City was like that for a while. I loved my friend that night, and the feeling of our time together created a bond that has lasted.

CHARLES STREET, New York City, May 1970

The man was good-looking enough, with red hair and an athletic build. My apartment was small; barely a mattress fit on the bedroom floor. It wasn't unusual to bring men there. Suddenly he pressed his mouth against mine and pushed me against a wall. This had never before happened. It took hours to get him to leave, and I was afraid. I whispered, "Please," in a voice that wasn't mine and I was surprised was so easily available. Maybe I got him to leave because I knew his cousin. I didn't tell her. I wish I had told her. After he left, I looked at the incident as a close call, and it changed nothing I can put my finger on about how I moved in the world. I considered it the kind of thing that didn't happen to me.

PATH Train, New Jersey, April 2008

After I returned from a gig in Chicago, I missed the last bus from the airport to New York. I was directed to a different bus. The driver of this one was beautiful with red lips. We cruised dark, sleepy streets, and I watched *Orange Is the New Black* on my phone. When we hit potholes, the bus sounded like a gun. All the other passengers were men. I wasn't tired. I waited for a PATH train with the men and got off at the World Trade Center, where I had to walk miles along secret corridors and up and down secret escalators to reach a subway train that crawled along the backbone of the city. I was back in my apartment by four thirty when the sky was turning light. I took a pill and watched *Veep*. What do you remember about your last dream?

DACHAU, Germany, July 1995

Yesterday my friend and I rode our bikes to the Munich U-Bahn at Marienplatz and waited for a train to Dachau. It has been hot for the past few days, and we were sticky from carrying our bikes down three flights of stairs. Our train arrived, and we passed through pleasant countryside on the brief journey. At Dachau, we carried our bikes outside and set off for the concentration camp about six kilometers from the center of the city, a ride through suburban streets and roads. It was over ninety degrees when we got there.

There was a small snack stand across from the camp. My friend asked if I wanted an ice cream before we entered, and I said I preferred to wait. The camp is on a main highway, not hidden. During the war, everyone in Dachau was aware of the camp, its functions, the state of the prisoners, the smell.

The place looked desolate and immaculate, with only two of the original barracks left standing. The building that had housed and trained officers had been turned into a museum. It was a large, U-shaped structure that included a theater, where we watched a film before starting the tour. Cleanliness and orderliness had been an obsession for the directors of concentration camps, so prisoners were confronted all the time with the contrast between the clean floors of the offices and the filth of their quarters. Four hundred people who were dirty and sick were crowded into buildings made to house sixty people.

Hitler assumed power in January 1933, and by March of that year Dachau had opened on the site of a former munitions factory. Arrests were made immediately of left-wing dissidents, priests, Roma, and Russians, in addition to Jews and homosexuals. Homosexuals were not mentioned in the film, nor were they discussed in the museum displays. The pink triangle was exhibited but not explained.

We visited the crematoria, two buildings set in the back of the camp. Someone had placed flowers in the mouth of one oven. I cried. I had teared up as well when we passed through the gate at the entrance. The place felt sanitized. It was called "A Memorial to Dachau." Sign after sign implored visitors to refrain from marking the walls. It was as if the German government still could not face its history. A few days earlier, I had been speaking with a woman who works with my friend, and she had complained about the harsh treatment Germans experience as a legacy of Nazism. She said, "People don't want to be associated with us. It's unjust. The French have Napoleon and no one hates them for that, but they won't stop hating us for Hitler." I thought, *Napoleon didn't mount a holocaust against Jews*, but I didn't say anything, and I don't speak German.

The captives at Dachau were used as slave labor. They were starved, beaten, and made to work in the quarries until they were skeletal and died. The crematoria were in use all the time because so many people were shot or killed in other ways. We entered a gas chamber, which, for some reason, had been built but not used at this camp.

Three chapels had been erected on the site in the 1960s. My friend, who is German, objected to them offering consolation to visitors while no consolation had been available to the prisoners. We saw a building where prisoners had been penned like animals and whipped routinely for leaving so much as a piece of straw on the swept floors. We saw "the whipping block." There was a whip secured across it with metal thongs. People were hung from metal hooks for hours and tortured by being made to stand in one place for many hours. In the museum, we saw the beautiful and horrified faces of so many people who were killed. My friend was bothered by a metal sculpture that suggested the skeletal shapes of the dead and dying that sat at the entrance to the U-shaped building. She thought it diminished the horror, as did trees that had been planted around the crematoria, suggesting a pastoral vista when none had existed at the time. I said a better place for the sculpture would be in the center of the town, Dachau, where no acknowledgment was made of what had happened there.

We left the camp and rode back to Munich, twelve miles or so. We had coffee and ice cream at a café. Then we walked up a hill to the old quarter through winding, picturesque streets, lined with expensive clothing shops and restaurants. That night, we went out with friends who served champagne. Everyone drinks champagne in Munich. A few nights later, at another dinner, my friend described our trip to

Dachau, and a woman at the table who was drunk and spoke in German I could more or less understand—especially the word *Juden*—said that, in addition to the Germans, many other people in Europe and America had wanted to see the power of Jewish financiers destroyed. My friend pointed out to the drunk woman that she was basically repeating Nazi propaganda. I said (in English) that the Jews who had been killed were largely not wealthy. I could see the woman was somewhere else. She felt stained by what had happened to the Jews in her country, and no matter what she did, she could not wash it off.

CHRISTIE'S, New York City, May 2006

I was catering in a small gallery, passing drinks. On display was a bisected sheep in a Plexiglas case made by Damien Hirst, and it looked the way everyone's life is going to go. The station where we picked up drinks was behind a black curtain. The way time works in catering, you forget about death.

Kathy Acker and Chris Kraus, or How to Write In a Way That Will Be Reviled until Everyone Will Read You as Necessary

Borges said the writing of Kafka was so original, it created its own precursors. It made us read Kierkegaard and the ninth-century Chinese writer Han Yu as Kafkaesque. Without Kafka, we would not notice their calm ability to make strangeness ordinary and the ordinary strange. The writing of Chris Kraus is so layered and witty, it is causing things to look Krausian. The best way to read the writing of Kathy Acker is as a precursor to the writing of Chris Kraus.

Acker still won't give you pleasure. No one, including Kraus, claims they feel pleasure reading Acker. In a recent phone conversation, Kraus said that, as an aspiring some-kind-of-artist in 1980s New York, she got high on Acker's chutzpah to place her own subjectivity at the center of her sentences. This Acker does, as well as her menstrual blood, bad fucks, ambition to be famous, torture porn, and rich-girl thefts from better writers to pay herself. On the phone, Kraus said, "I would see her at an art opening or a party, and my palms would get sweaty, and I'd be frozen with awe and terror." Years later, Kraus reports in the autofiction *I Love Dick* (1997) she was browsing through the books of Sylvère Lotringer, whom she would marry, and found a volume inscribed, *To Sylvère, The Best Fuck In The World (At Least To My Knowledge) Love, Kathy Acker*. So, there is that link too.

In 1997, Acker died in a Tijuana alternative health facility at age fifty, from breast cancer she chose not to treat with chemotherapy. Five or so years later, Kraus thought of writing a biography of Acker but hesitated, sensing she didn't have the detachment she would need to find a story worth telling and a voice to tell it in. The story worth telling could not celebrate Acker's artistry, although there is daring and invention in what she wrote. She was an avatar of the great Lower East Side, do-it-yourself art camp, where anyone can put on a show in a hole in the wall café and anyone can be an artist with a patchwork of found objects.

Acker spliced her letters and diary entries between slabs of appropriated texts from Dickens, Propertius, Emily Brontë, and scads of others, producing surprising formal effects and willing her experience into the body of Literature. No detail of corporeal existence was out-of-bounds. She could be rude, occasionally funny, and stark. Sentences here and there jump out with simple truth and wit. "Intense sexual desire is the greatest thing in the world (*Eurydice in the Underworld*)." "Murderers know nothing about fashion (*My Mother: Demonology*)".

Still, overall, the writing is dull in its sameness. The narrators look in, not out. They feel, feel, feel, but we do not see, see, see what they are looking at. Their pronouncements are melodramatic, their images overblown. They ask for love, a pat on the head for their erudition, and agreement with their analyses and summaries. It's exhausting to keep having to say okay.

Wisely, Kraus turned her attention to the circus of Acker's life and to her disciplined march to a place in the world. Wikipedia lists twenty-six published titles in Acker's entry. By the time she was thirty-two, she was the subject of an hour-long documentary as part of the prestigious British *The South Bank Show*. She began by self-publishing and eventually formed a relationship with Grove Press. She became a literary superstar in '80s England and in the States and elsewhere a punk-glam luminary, performing onstage to large, appreciative crowds, marketing herself as a gender outlaw with her tattooed, pierced biker body and Comme des Garçon clothes.

She lived like a man without bearing children; she lived like a woman by putting her body at risk of pregnancy and having five abortions. She lived like a man by ignoring women; she lived like a woman by focusing on men. She lived like a man by putting work at the center of her life; she lived like a woman by asking men to advance her career. She was the smartest girl in any room, her hand darting up to answer all the questions and nab all the boyfriends. If you, too, were a cannibal, Kathy would eat your friends and then eat you.

In *After Kathy Acker*, Kraus nails this persona as a crafted calculation:

> Just as the twenty-three-year-old Acker trained herself to heighten the emotional pitch of her diary by deleting conjunctions and adjectives, throughout her life she consistently sought situations that would result in disruptive intensity for all parties involved. Almost all the emotional tributes and essays penned in the wake of her death by friends speak of her 'vulnerability'. Yet, like most of the rest of her writing and life, her vulnerability was highly strategic. Pursuing a charged state of grace, Acker knew, in some sense, *exactly* what she was doing. To pretend otherwise is to discount the crazed courage and breadth of her work.

After Kathy Acker is a brilliant meditation on female ambition in the second half of the twentieth century.

Note to humans: do not stop writing, even when you are suffering from an STD, recovering from an abortion, pining for the most recent schmendrick who, after that morning's fuck, cast dead eyes upon the space above your head. Kraus's book is fun, fun, fun. It reads like a performance monologue you don't want to end, layered with her trademark descriptive powers, exhaustive research, personal revelations, and gossipy eyewitness accounts of the Downtown scene.

Like Acker, Kraus is interested in the female body and the female mind in a world that reviles them. Like Acker, Kraus is interested more generally in power granted and power denied. And Kraus, too, combines genres with anarchic flare, but where Acker is pounding, abstract, and grandiose, Kraus is comic, speculative, and compassionate.

With typical fluidity, Kraus here sketches the freewheeling dance scene of the 1970s and Acker's intersection with it:

> Soon after arriving back in New York [in 1976], she discovered the open dance/movement classes that were held in loft studios with wood floors and huge rattling windows, in apartments and theater spaces rented on an hourly basis by soon-to-be-legendary dancer/choreographers Simone Forti, Trisha Brown, and Kenneth King. No formal dance steps were taught. . . . King shared

Acker's background in philosophy and Latin. His 'grid dances'... must have seemed to Acker like an embodied analogue to her own texts.... Acker embraced the community's grueling regime of back-to-back classes preceded by two hours of yoga and followed by marathon jams.

Most enjoyably, *After Kathy Acker* is a love letter to all the sexually abject, bookish, hungry girls who have ever looked for a way to get to the party, and it invites you to the party you wish you had been cool enough to attend in the first place. Kraus forms a bridge to Acker, even arousing tenderness for a person who, by all accounts, was as self-centered and demanding in life as her narrators are on the page.

In *I Love Dick*, Kraus writes, "What happens between women now is the most interesting thing in the world because it's least described." Kraus looks out. Acker tries to make an impression. In *My Mother: Demonology* (1993), she does a mash-up between her personal writing and *Wuthering Heights*, taking on the role of brooding, sadistic Heathcliff, who has been abused as a child. Kraus, on the other hand, echoes the rebellion at the heart of *Jane Eyre*. When Charlotte Brontë's sisters, Emily and Anne, warned her that no one would read a book about a heroine who was plain, Charlotte said, in effect, *Just watch me*. Kraus says the same thing in everything she writes. (In reality, she is quite attractive, but her narrators call themselves "hags." We feel what we feel about our bodies.)

Acker strove to be singular and to become a star. When she controls the narrative of her life, we see cartoons, meat, and pain. The power of Kraus's eye is in the way it looks at Acker as an example of a collective condition. By focusing on Acker's desires—whether fulfilled or thwarted—Kraus is in her element, and Acker becomes human.

Suppose, Kraus invites us to imagine, you are a waify, Jewish girl who does not think she is pretty, and who other kids think has cooties and smells bad and does smell bad because her parents don't notice how often she bathes and do not trouble themselves to buy her nice clothes. Suppose you are a girl who reads all the time and carries her books with the spines out so everyone can see she is poring over Dostoevsky, Gogol, and Turgenev. Suppose your mother does not love you and your father has left before you were born. Your mother will commit suicide in a hotel, rather than learn to spend less money on clothes and food. Suppose you mistake sexual desire for interest in you and you discover you like sex—or at least seducing people—because it makes you feel connected and powerful in a way you will never put your finger on. Suppose you feel rejected almost as soon as sex is over, and you become a student of abjectness, turning the subject this way and that in various lights. Suppose you find a voice by combining your love of books with the subject of sexual abjectness, and suppose you observe that males have power. You situate yourself with them; identify with them; get them to teach you; introduce you to people with jobs, money, places to stay, because males have been trained to say yes to almost anything a female asks if he thinks he will get laid.

In Kraus's rich account, the story of Acker is also the story of Kraus and the story of all women who will continue to scratch at the gate until the gate has been burned down. For all Acker's cyberpunk stylings, she comes off as a throwback to Mary McCarthy and Susan Sontag, women who wanted to be glittering exceptions rather than runners in a pack. Everywhere in Acker's surround the women's movement was rethinking how women are represented and how women represent themselves. Acker did not engage in such organized activism. In terms of creating an alternative female model, she was inventing fire in her own small room, while outside crowds had already built a bonfire.

What makes a book? Whatever wakes up desire—and not necessarily good romance. This is what both Kraus and Acker believe. Kraus goes further. In her work, she turns the idiom of *Fatal Attraction* on its head. Recall that in the movie, Alix, the opera-loving predator, is meant to be a monster. In the literature of Kraus (and Acker), the fevered, infatuated stalker/lover is the hero, and every man is at risk of finding the family bunny cooked in a pot. And why not? Who wants to wait to be chosen when it is never going to happen?

Friend

My friend N used to tell a story about a cat she was minding that died in her care. N also had a cat at the time, and these two cats did not get along. They had to be separated, so when the visiting cat came to stay with N, it was placed in a room by itself, and in a way I don't remember the cat was killed by something falling on it, maybe, or by crawling into a space it couldn't get out of. The way N told the story, you would fall on the floor laughing: the cat's surprising death, her horror at discovering the stiff corpse, what she imagined she would tell the friend, and the trouble she had getting the cat cremated.

She didn't tell her friend the whole truth, as I recall, some details were left out, and I think the friend had also been a former girlfriend, which maybe added or didn't add to the predicament N found herself in, and I don't recall, either, whether the cat's death hastened the demise of their relationship, although it may have. From time to time, I would ask N to do her nightclub routine about the dead cat so I could laugh. She didn't crack a smile, and this impressed me, because I will always ruin a story by laughing at it myself.

The story you are reading is about the end of my friendship with N, an ending that also involves the death of an animal. This animal was a dog that for a long time belonged to a woman N knew slightly or knew in the distant past, before this woman turned up in N's life, dying. N could not pass a deathbed without gluing herself to it, and she would tell herself she was really close to the person or had been, even though I don't think it was often the case. I think N was studying death and couldn't get enough of it, like those grave robbers in earlier centuries who needed bodies to cut up in order to see how they worked. N would sign herself onto a death crew, visiting the sick person every day and consulting with doctors and social workers—anything to ease the dying person's end—and, in this case, promising to adopt the woman's Yorkshire terrier, who was not in her first youth. I resented N's random generosity because it seemed to devalue her generosity toward me, which I expected to flow in my direction until one of us died.

N was the colleague of R, a close friend of mine, so N and I would see each other from time to time before becoming friends on our own. She was a professor of French literature, but her deeper love was painting, and one day I received an invitation to a show of her work and was bowled over. She painted figures, mostly portraits, and at this time the faces and nude bodies of very old women, which were startling and bold and very accomplished, owing something to the way Lucian Freud made paint appear to be skin.

We became friends just after the death of Gardner, a man I had been with for a long time, who was also a painter. N and I quickly became a kind of couple. It was friendship the way friendship is portrayed in *Sex and the City*, as an alternative to family. It was friendship the way it was idealized in the hopeful and baseless theories produced by feminists like me. I was forty-four when Gardner died. N is seven years older than me.

At the beginning, when we were speaking on the phone most days, or walking from this gallery opening to that party, or flopping on her bed to watch something on her small TV, she was traveling back and forth to California to spend time with yet another woman who was dying. This one had been her girlfriend for a number of years and made N feel known and loved beyond what anyone else could stir in her, and when this woman died, N felt a hole in her life she didn't know how to fill. I had started a hot affair with a man that, in earth time, quickly spiraled down but about whom I sorrowed for years and, even now, can still taste if I reach into the back of my throat-mind. N was the best person in the world for such a situation. For both of us, relationships were impossible states of hell. We went out of our minds fast, the way in each of us as well anger could flash.

Everywhere I look these days, I see people trying to improve themselves as moral individuals, and it bores me. I'm trying to accept that, to many people, I've proved unreliable. My mother used to say of me, "A leopard never changes its spots." She meant I couldn't be trusted to place loyalty to the family—and to her—above my wish to be loved by the world. When I ask myself, How are you doing with this project of accepting yourself as a person who harms and irritates other people? My answer is: I'm getting nowhere. One of the things I loved about N is that we could yell at each other in frustration and accusation, Jew to Jew, then cool off and be okay, without even leaving the room. This is something that will never happen between me and the man I live with now, and with whom it is impossible to be Jew to Jew, and who in fact wishes I would never raise my voice. That he wishes this and that I know I cannot grant his wish, although it is reasonable and probably even good, is how I know my mother was right, and I kind of miss her, not to mention N.

N and I were about the same size, although she thought she was bigger, and she prided herself on being able to use tools. During the 1960s and early 1970s, when the rest of us were plotting to upend the universe with regard to who got to do things, while the rest of us were marching for this cause and that cause, N was building a house from scratch with her own hands on top of a hill in upstate New York. Five million times, she said, as if for the first time, "I would drive up to the house every Friday and start working so fast, I didn't even close the car door."

As a consequence of "missing out on the sixties," as she put it, she quit teaching after the attacks of 9/11 and became a full-time activist on behalf of women's rights in the Middle East. She quit painting, too, or painting quit her. I remember walking around Lower Manhattan with her. We were on our way to a party for a book or something, going for the free food and drinks and a reason to walk and talk. It started to rain before we got there, and we ducked into the lobby of a building with marble walls and tiny tiles on the floor like a Roman mosaic. She said, "Should I take early retirement?" I said, "Yes." *Yes* was the way you got from point A to point B.

In recent years, she'd been in love with a woman who was married to a man. It went on and on with excitement and hand-wringing until it turned into the kind of friendship that always had a toothache. Scholarship had not been a great interest of N's. She'd loved working with students but was ready to kick away her life. She told me about the money she had saved and the money that would be coming to her when she retired and the difference between that money and the money she would receive if she went on teaching a few more years. I said, "Do what your heart tells you to do." Inside the field of human rights activism on behalf of women and girls, she organized shelters, saved lives, changed laws. And she missed nothing about the life she had lived before. Including me.

I was the person you were supposed to call, we'd agreed, if something happened to her, and I helped her home after this outpatient procedure or that one. She called me Laurski. She had a mother she loved and a father she had been afraid to come out to. I don't remember if she came out to him before he died. She had thick, dark hair she cut in the shape of topiaries. She liked to wear my clothes. When I was catering parties and needed extra hands, she jumped in, regardless of the task. She thought it was fun. It was fun. She liked whatever I cooked for her. She made the absolute best popcorn. I made the absolute best margaritas.

When I was hit by a car on my bike, riding to meet her at yet another party, she was the one who came and loaded me and my bike into a cab. When I needed to have my knee reconstructed and stayed in the hospital for a few days, she helped me set up the machine that moved my knee so it wouldn't freeze. She installed a pedestal sink in my bathroom and track lights throughout my apartment. She rebuilt the closet in my bedroom so it could accommodate Gardner's art. She gave me notes on everything I wrote. She was a good reader if the writing made sense to her. Not everything I wrote was intended to make sense. When I had a facelift, she picked me up at the doctor's office and spent the night applying bags of frozen peas to my sutures. The next morning, I looked practically normal.

We both had stories of friendships that had come undone, and we told them to each other as a way to knock wood about ours. N would recall this one who had stopped talking to her or that one she had cut out of her life, staring off, her face going slack or pale, as if watching herself go over a cliff or seeing someone in a crash sprawled out on a road. Everyone who knew her, even briefly, knew it was very hard for her to say the word *no*, so people asked her to take care of animals, read books in the works, donate money to causes, put up their friends in her apartment or house. I didn't believe she would ever say no to me in a way that was final.

A question: In the women's movement, when we found ourselves attached to friends instead of family, what did we mean by trust? Trust to do what? Trust to not do what? Anyone who learns to conceal a secret self knows how to break a bond of trust when it's in the way of something else you want. Doesn't everyone learn to conceal a secret self inside family life? Inside any relationship?

I don't think of betrayal as such a terrible thing when I look at what human beings are. By human beings, I mean me. I don't trust anyone, really, not to let go of me. I don't think anyone trusts me not to let go of them, even though I've seldom let go of people I've loved. Once, after my break with N, she answered a call I made, and she squeezed out a few sentences in a voice like sandpaper. I said, "I'm happy to hear you." She said, "I'm not happy to hear you." I said, "Don't you miss us?" She said, "At first, but not now." She said, "I don't trust you," or maybe she said, "I can never trust you." She said, "You don't even know what you did." I said, "Tell me." She wouldn't say more. I don't think of betrayal as such a terrible thing when I'm the one doing the betraying.

It's been more than four years since our friendship ended. We didn't speak all the years of Trump, all the time my sister was sick and died. I wrote to N about my sister, and she didn't call me. If the dead-sister card didn't work, N isn't coming back. When you learn you are dead to someone, it's as if you have died and you go on in a kind of half-life.

N had sex with people who were married. She badgered people she worked with to agree with her sense of right and wrong, and if they didn't agree, she badgered them more. I miss her. The number of times we laughed: a million. She would burst into a staggered honk, her mouth open like the mask of comedy, her eyebrows through the roof. The number of times I heard N say *I'm sorry* to anyone: zero. The amount it's helped me in life trying to understand why people do the things they do: also zero.

I don't remember the prompt that produced the first piece I wrote about N's dog, the little Yorkie she adopted from the woman who died, the Yorkie that sometimes smelled bad and had bad teeth and, as it got older, the thickened, pearly eyes of a zombie. Could the prompt have been something as innocuous as "write about an animal"? Or "write about a relationship between a person and an animal"? For a few weeks after adopting the dog, N felt saddled, but there was a tipping point. We were at a fabulous party in Brooklyn with views of the river, and there was great food and drinks and smart, interesting people around. It was a book party for a friend of mine, and suddenly N announced she had to get home to the dog. The dog would be lonely or need her in some way. That night, I walked across the Brooklyn Bridge with a man I went to have drinks with and never saw again.

N took the dog everywhere in a backpack she wore. She talked about the dog the way people talk about the person they are in love with. People got tired of the dog or enjoyed the dog. The dog was N's kid and best friend. The dog lived for another eight years. I like dogs, but not this one. It had a ratty, insistent quality. As it got older, it developed a loud cough that sounded as if it were choking. The problem couldn't be fixed. Whatever could be fixed, N tried to fix. When we traveled, it came with us.

One day, after the dog died, I decided to work on the little piece I'd sketched, and it turned into a story, a funny story that was kind of mean, although not as mean as it would need to be in order to work as a story. It was as tiny as the dog, maybe three hundred and fifty words. The narrator relates the dog's death, which was pretty much based on what really happened. What really happened is the dog was becoming frail and unresponsive during a time I was staying with N in her apartment in the Village because outside my apartment on the Upper West Side construction was going on to build a giant high-rise. N placed the dog in the basket of her bike and rode it a mile or so uptown to her vet and returned with the dog wrapped in a yellow blanket. Only the dog was no longer alive at this point, and N wasn't sure and asked me to check.

In real life, I checked and sure enough, the dog was dead, its tongue hanging limply from its jagged mouth, and I had to tell N, who was in another room, leaning against a wall. I held her and felt sad for her and the dog. She was so distraught, you would have needed a heart of stone not to feel for her grief and feel grief, too, for the starkness of death beside us.

When I wrote the story as it had happened, it sounded sentimental and seemed to betray the joyful malice the narrator feels toward her rival and fellow stray. So I flipped it. I wrote something I had not felt. In the story, the narrator, finally rid of the bloody animal, confides to the reader: "It was all I could do to keep from laughing."

I used to say to N I thought I was basically a moral person, except when it came to sex. I would sleep with people who weren't free, and I would lie to the people

I was with by not telling them what I'd done. It turns out I am a lot less upstanding than that. I will please myself at the expense of others. I do not purposely try to hurt people, but I am willing, it appears, to sacrifice their interests and sense of trust in me if it stands in the way of something I want. That's who I am. That's who I've been. It surprises me that more people are not writing these exact sentences all the time.

During the first few years of my estrangement from N, I thought it was because I had delivered a painful truth to her. I had said she seemed to be losing mental acuity. For years, I had been noticing moments of forgetfulness and confusion, and I thought maybe there was something she could do about it. We were together at her house in the country, the one she'd built by hand, and she'd forgotten important facts about a friend of hers. She'd forgotten this friend had been worried she'd had cancer. It turned out she didn't have cancer, but N didn't remember any of it, even though she'd gone to stay with the woman for a week in Boston while the woman awaited the result of tests.

It hadn't been that long ago. And as we sat there, I told her about other incidents that worried me—times she had left me waiting at train stations, although we'd gone over my time of arrival, a time very late at night I had picked her up at an airport and she had wandered around for over an hour without her cell phone. There was more I kept back.

She became angry and denied anything was wrong. She pretended to remember the incident about her friend's cancer scare. I don't think she remembered it at all. From then on, if she got lost on a route she'd driven hundreds of times, or searched for a word, or lost her train of thought midsentence, all she had to do was look at my face to feel herself dissolving into a black hole. Who would not want to exit from that?

I still believe that's why she let go of me, but I don't know and I don't blame her. I pulled away first, actually. Four years ago, she said on the phone I had lied to her about having car insurance, even though I owned a car and could not drive the car without the kind of insurance that covers the driver in any car they drive. Even though I gave her the number of my policy and she called the company, she wasn't satisfied and believed I had been lying to her for years. I sent her a text saying I couldn't be spoken to this way anymore and left the set of keys I had to her apartment and some shirts of hers in a shopping bag by her front door. Neither of us communicated for a year, maybe?

It was the longest we'd gone without speaking. I missed her and sent an email or two. Nothing. I left a voicemail saying I was thinking about her and hoped we could be in touch. Nothing. I couldn't understand it. She'd resumed with people after a lot angrier business than the thing about the car insurance. She picked up the phone once or twice when I called after that, and a few times my phone rang and I saw her name, and when I said hello, she sounded confused and said she had called by mistake. Her friends would not speak to me about what was going on. Not one of them believed anything was wrong with her memory. They said it was ordinary aging.

A year and a half ago, I spent an afternoon with our mutual friend, R, the man who'd introduced us. We went to a small park uptown, near where we both lived. He said, "It wasn't the car. It was the dog." He meant the story I'd written about N's dog and that, at the last minute, I'd added to the manuscript of *My Life as an Animal, Stories*.

Why did I do that? I thought the mean/funny story added something real to the book. But what did I think would happen when N read it? I didn't think she'd read it because she'd already read the manuscript so many times. But what if she did read it? I thought she'd fume and get over it; it wouldn't break our bond. I'd say I really *had* felt sad when the dog died. I'd *lied* to write a better story, which was the truth. I'd say,

"The narrator compares herself to the dog. They're both strays. The joke is as much at the expense of the bedraggled narrator as the dog."

The truth is, reader, I didn't think about how N would feel when she read the story. Thinking about her feelings might have stopped me, and I didn't want to be stopped. That is the nature of a course of action like mine. You act and apologize later if you have to. You try to make it up to the person you've hurt. You still get what you wanted to get, assuming it isn't the end of everything.

R and I were beside a little fountain. I'd been pleased at the prospect of seeing him. I could see he wasn't pleased to see me. He said, "She bought ten copies of your book to give to people. They called her and said, 'Did you see the story about the dog?'" I said, "Oh, god. How awful." He said, "She felt like a fool." Then a weird thing happened: I felt hopeful. It was like finding out tests for a diagnosis had been wrong, and you still had time. Now that I knew why she wouldn't talk to me, I could write her a letter of apology and say I hadn't really been happy when the dog died, although in absolute candor, reader, it was a relief not to hear its hacking cough any longer or see its terrifying eyes.

If I had to do it again, I would not have included the story in the book without telling N. She might have hated me for writing it, but she wouldn't have been blindsided. That, perhaps, she could have forgiven. She didn't respond to the letter of apology. Maybe the story of the dog was the excuse she was looking for to let me go. People you know for a long time grow burdensome and tedious. The disparity between her generosity to me and mine to her was laughably large.

If I had to do it again, I would have still written the story. It is funny the way the story of the dead cat is funny. N would not have told the story of the dead cat to the owner of the cat the way she had crafted it for everyone else. She wouldn't have told her the story at all, which is why I didn't want to show N the story of the dead dog. A friend of mine recently saw N and learned she'd had COVID and now attributed the fog in her thinking to the virus. She said they'd had dinner and some of the time N had seemed as sharp as she'd always been.

A glass vase N bought for one of my birthdays sits on a window in my apartment. I don't go there much these days. I'm thinking of bringing it to Hudson, so when I see it, I can remember N sitting across from me in her apartment, each of us on one of the armchairs she'd built by hand, drinking margaritas and laughing about something ridiculous we didn't want to end, laughing about the way we can never know ourselves.

Why am I telling you this story? Haven't I just done it again—exposed N's life without asking her permission? I try to follow three directives when I write: don't apologize, don't translate yourself, and don't ask for love. I wonder if I am asking for your love, reader, even though in life, you could not love me if I wrote a story about your dead dog. Or maybe even N's dead dog. Were she to read this, would she feel betrayed all over again? I wrote with the freedom of knowing she would never take me back. You may think I am asking you to take me back, and I always am, and you can't. If N read this, she would see it's a love letter.

Catering

My friend P said, "I know you write about catering, but do you really know how to do it?" I said, "Yes." He said, "I want to have a party for D. He's going to be fifty. People will be flying in. I want live music, and a sit-down dinner, and dancing with a DJ. We'll have it at the house by the ocean. Where do I start?" I said, "You need a planner—someone to order rental, hire staff, arrange flowers, decide on a menu and drinks, a cake, lights, a dance floor, a tent if it rains." He said, "Where do I get a planner?" I said, "Oy." He said, "Help me." I said, "I love you." And I could feel that pull to the not-think I am often looking for. Catering, you're on your feet twelve hours. A sip of champagne. A bite of crabmeat in a fried wonton skin. A swirl of icing slid off the knife. Ten miles walking. Your mind empty as the air above June surf.

I got fired from the *Voice* when I was fifty-three. I was ready to leave. A door closes; a great jagged gap in your inner life opens. I was never ready to leave. It was

1999. I had been writing for the paper since 1974. As a writer for the *Voice*, I was offered gigs to travel and write. There was always free food. This didn't happen so much afterward.

At the time I was fired, Don Forst was running the paper, and Doug Simmons was his deputy. They were asking writers and editors to work more for less pay— for example to write columns as part of their salaried jobs, instead of, as always, for an extra fee. I said this was wrong to a rival paper, and the next day I was called into Don's office and told to leave. I floated past desks and faces for the last time. I'd biked from the Upper West Side to Cooper Square, and I rode back along the river, unable to see or hear.

After I got off the phone with P, I said to the man I live with, "I agreed to do the party." He said, "Have fun." I said, "P is putting us up at a hotel for two nights. It's on the ocean. You love the ocean." He said, "I won't wear an apron, or a vest, or a hat." I said, "Fine." He said, "I don't like talking to strangers." I said, "That's the beauty of working instead of being a guest. You don't have to talk to anyone."

After I left the *Voice*, the thought of being a regular freelance writer who would accept assignments and send out proposals to who-knows-who and to people who didn't know me or want my style the way it already was, the thought of doing any of this and scrabbling together a living the way zillions of writers did in those days—the thought of this was just *no*. Writers were threading themselves into creative writing programs at universities. Creative writing programs were replicating in vats like in *The Matrix*. I didn't see myself on a faculty. I didn't want to teach. I thought maybe I could come to these places as a guest whatever and give a workshop and a reading and talk about my experiences as a writer. The internet was up and running, and there were websites with links you could email to.

To my amazement, there was interest from several programs, and while I was setting up visits, I called my friend Julie and told her I wanted to become a cater-waiter, and could she ask her friend Spencer if I could work for his company? She said, "Why do you want to be a cater-waiter?" She sounded sad. I said, "I like being around food. I think I want to use my body instead of my mind." She said, "The pay's not great." I said, "It will only be for a few months."

It makes me anxious to tell you this part of the story because I didn't know what I was doing and, in telling you this part of the story, I can taste the fog I was in and the way I have maybe always misplaced the names of my emotions so I could wake up in the morning and face the mirror. I think I was stricken by grief. I think I was shocked by being let go of so easily. I think it reminded me I was a leaf, or I felt like a leaf, and like a leaf I wafted this way and that. I didn't know I was bereft. Everyone else knew I was bereft and a little pathetic and abject. Everyone else could see what I couldn't see, the same as always. Everyone's life is a TV show you forget other people are watching.

A few things you can put together if you like. (These things will come together even if you don't put them together, because that's the human response to a list.) I didn't really need the money. At the time, I was buying and selling stocks. It was the dot-com era, and I could have managed without what I earned from catering. I disliked working for the company Spencer owned because it was structured on a military model with newbies at the bottom, doing the heavy lifting of moving tables and bagging chairs, and lifers, burnished with resentment, drifting off to the bathrooms and hallways because it was their right. I disliked the company but stuck it out until friendly waiters clued me to companies where the staff was collegial and the management not a bunch of bitter fucks.

One night, it turned out the event I had come to work at was the annual gala for PEN America, the writers' organization I belong to. I was offered a job out of sight of the guests. I chose instead to weave in and out of people I knew, dressed in a tux and carrying trays. I thought by doing this, I would have something to write about, and I did write about the night in a piece called "Report from the Food Chain." In it, the narrator—that is, I—dissolves inside the sense of failure and exile that, in a sense, I staged. I didn't know I had staged it at the time. It's unclear what the piece is about. People liked the colorful, physical details of catering. Visual details are a gift to any piece of writing.

Over the years, I have worked in the homes of billionaires. (Very rich people are not known for generous tips.) I have worked shoulder to shoulder with a few renowned chefs. I learned the right way to cut anything. I loved the actors and dancers and aspiring whatevers I worked with. I didn't want to quit working with them in a team. I didn't want to feel lost and lonely on my own. If the job I was assigned didn't require moving all the time—such as checking coats—I would refuse to do it. I didn't stop calling bookers for catering jobs, even though it meant running into people I knew in other parts of my life and who sometimes stared at me, frozen in place and unable to speak. Most of the people I know have said to me, in one way or another, "I could do X or Y to make money, but I could never take a service job and wait on people."

Over the years, the man I live with has prepped ingredients when I have been hired to cook. We hadn't been together long when he agreed (under hostage conditions) to prepare the batter for madeleines and bake off several pans for Christmas dinners I'd booked. He knows how to unpack rental and set it up—clothing tables, unwrapping glasses and silverware, stocking a bar. At the party we did for N, he placed votive candles inside white sandwich bags, creating "lanterns" he set along the walks.

A week before the party, I ran the kind of fever you get only as a kid, and my brain went to mush. We figured it was Lyme disease—it would turn out to be a different tickborne disease called anaplasmosis—and I started taking doxycycline. At the time I had poison ivy as well that was mistakenly diagnosed by a doctor as an allergic reaction to the doxy. I was down, and then I was up. There was no way I was going to fail N. And I didn't. The man I live with and I pulled it off, with the help of two young men hired to serve and the others hired for their gigs.

We arrived a day early to set up the rental, and the day of the party, we were on our feet for thirteen hours straight. The rain that had threatened fell. The guests moved under the tent. The moon splashed the waves. The cake was layered with whipped cream and blueberry jam. A jazz quartet played Ellington. The DJ played Talking Heads. And I remembered the way, at parties, we'd danced after the guests had left, turning up the volume and feeling happy to be alone with each other. The young were happy to be young. I was happy to be alive.

It's hard for me to turn down a catering job, and I doubt I will in the future while I can still run around and keep my wits about me, making this or that decision on the spur—*take the cake out of the fridge, replenish the Thai salad, refill the water glasses!* Before the start of P's party, I said to him, "I won't be the Laurie you are used to. I will be nicer. My job is to give you a good party, and the only thing that makes a party good is the pleasure of the guests." It's hard for me to turn down a catering job because I am good at the work and because it's laced, ineluctably, with a sense of lostness floating on motion.

This is not a story about making lemonade pie from lemons. This is not a story about lemons. Everything I do is stirred by a frisson of exile and aloneness because that is who I am. It's neither okay nor not okay. It just is.

DENOUEMENT

New York City

Postcard to Ann Snitow (1943–2019)

Dear Ann,

I am remembering the signs we made so often at your loft on Spring Street. One year, you wanted a certain color. When asked to describe it, you said, "Prada green," and I thought I should know what that color was, and I found it in a magazine—a key lime pie green shot through a bolt of electricity. One time in the 1970s, I was on a panel you organized, maybe at the Gay and Lesbian Center on 13th Street, and to introduce us you said we believed in "the social construction of gender." I had not heard that phrase before. I said, "What's that?" and you looked at me with compassion for my ignorance and said, "Oh, it means we don't think biology determines our lives. We think people make up ideas about masculinity and femininity that can be changed." I said, "Oh, yes, I believe that," and you moved on to your next thought.

Last night I was talking with our mutual friend, S, and she said, "I always wanted to hear what Ann would say. She would listen to others present arguments, and then, when it was her turn to speak, she would find the beautiful bits in what she'd heard and put it all back together in a way that was brilliant and original and made people think she was extending their ideas."

I googled you after you died, and a *New Yorker* piece popped up about Shulamith Firestone, who wrote *The Dialectic of Sex* (1970)—one of the axis-tilting books of the movement—and was a founding member of New York Radical Women, Redstockings, and New York Radical Feminists. In the article, you are quoted as calling her "incandescent" and saying, "It was thrilling to be in her company." That's so like you. Pretty much everyone else in the essay gripes about how difficult she was, and the piece is depressing to read, not only because Firestone went mad after her book became a hit and later died one of those emaciated bag-lady feminist deaths, alone and penniless, but because it described the awful fractiousness in the early days of the women's movement, where, if you signed your name to a piece of writing, other women called you an egomaniac—and worse, said you were acting like a man.

The piece brought back that time, which lives still in our current wave of hall monitors and head girls, picking at terms and prefixes as if separating peas from fried rice. The piece brought back that time because it had drifted into the mists. When I think about the meetings and marches and seminars and fundraisers I've attended in the last four decades, mostly at the center is you, a woman who thought more was more and who scorned only the concept of scorning.

I entered the women's movement when I entered adult life. They are the same thing to me. Kate Millett was my teacher at Barnard, and she swept me into her orbit—not me especially; all of her students—but some of us lingered around her office door, the way fans do at stage doors, and were invited down to her loft on Bowery and First Street, where she would cook us steaks.

The minute you become a feminist—and I think it takes a minute, don't you?—all the language used to describe everything in the world sounds false. It sounds thin and wrong, and what are you going to do? Argue with every word? I would, honestly, but the language of argument is kind of boring to me, so you have to figure out a way to exist in the world that to you is Bizarro World, while your world, the world shared by other feminists, is the real world hardly anyone knows about. The way to live in Bizarro World and not go nuts or waste your existence in rage is what you gave me a map to—me and every other person who fell under your spell. You said, *Come. We will do things and eat something. We will drink something and talk about how to create more space in existence for women, and that is how we will get through life.*

You called me *darling*. You called everyone *darling*. I took it personally. I showed up at your place with friends who knew you. I showed up with the girls from *The Village Voice*—Ellen Willis, Karen Durbin, Cindy Carr, Sonia Robbins, Alisa Solomon, Erika Munk. In the group that was called "No More Nice Girls"—formed in the 1980s during the feminist sex wars and the larger war on women's bodily sovereignty—we marched against goodgirlitis. After one Iraq war or another, we formed "Take Back the Future" for street actions and "Feminist Futures" for reports from the front of gender studies. Always, you were designing costumes with bras and chains and dance moves to accompany drumming. Always, you were laughing your smart laugh at the dilemma at the core of feminism: that women were a thing devised by false understandings of them and yet, banded together to question this category mistake, they became a thing of their own devising.

I showed up for you, attracted by personal chemistry and a pressure to remake all understandings. Feminism was the great romance of our lives.

A year ago, at your loft, we sat together and talked. You had thrown a party to celebrate the new book of a poet friend. You said you wanted to spend the time you had left finishing your book about the Network of East-West Women, the organization you founded after the fall of the Berlin Wall, in order to open a conversation with women in that part of the world. We were on the roof in the garden. Walking up the stairs was not easy for you. You were telling me about the trees and plants blooming around us. You looked beautiful.

Children ran up and you cooed at them. Other friends tried to draw you away. I wanted your attention. I still believed in what Firestone had written in *The Dialectic of Sex*: "The end goal of feminist revolution must be . . . not just the elimination of male privilege but of the sex distinction itself: genital difference between human beings would no longer matter culturally." I think you believed this as well, but you stayed in conversation with people who thought feminism was about securing better tampons and preserving virginity for as long as possible. You rolled your eyes describing the mansplaining you witnessed at Occupy Wall Street meetings during the fall of 2011, and still you went.

Some things have been rattling around in my head I wish I could talk to you about. In the past, when we went into the streets, it felt like we were in conversation with a government, however repugnant its policies. We thought we could actually produce change, and we did: Johnson decided not to run again. Nixon resigned. Abortion became a legal right. Now, marching feels like running the old game with the old rules, when none of this exists anymore. It feels like accepting some kind of framework where oligarchic feudal terrorism is considered a government and we stand for that government's tolerance of protest. I kind of know what you would say. You'd say, "I see your point, darling, but we have to do it anyway," and then you would sigh one of your luxurious Weltschmerz sighs.

Your absence is not the loss of a single person. It's the loss of a wave, a home for the wayward and unanchored, a form of doing politics that is the same as doing the rest of life. You were very smart and funny, and I thought you could see right through whatever falseness was in front of you but didn't have the time to waste on not loving what there was to love.

That day in your garden, the sun was on your skin. You were worried you wouldn't get your book done. My sister's death was fresh. I said, "You will finish your book." The other day, your friend, S, recalled the way you dealt with the phone. You would wait to hear who was calling, then pick up if the person was someone you needed to speak to. The rest you would call back after 4:00 p.m., if you wanted to call them back at all. You didn't watch TV. I said to S, "What was she doing instead of talking on the phone and watching TV?"— two of my favorite activities. S said, "She was reading, writing, preparing her classes, doing all the organizing and organizing and organizing." You thought there was never enough time to do the things you wanted to do, and you were right, and still I wanted to keep you in your chair, talking to me.

Give Peas a Chance

The father of a friend died recently, and she sent me an obit he wrote, published in a local paper. He was ninety-one and knew he was dying. He'd done lots of things of use in the world and felt much pleasure, and he said being bisexual had opened his life in the ways he valued most. Above all, he said, feeling love had been the best part of life. As in, "All you need is love." As in, John and Yoko's Bed-Ins for Peace in the 1960s.

Reading the obit made me happy. What a great way to look back on a life! Then I remembered I love hating. Or am good at it. Who knows the difference.

The other day, I came across a piece I'd performed in Lower Manhattan a few weeks after the planes hit the Towers in 2001. We were in a space without electricity—the power hadn't come back on yet—at an event organized by Dixon Place. In the piece, I compared myself to the Taliban as a way to understand why the Taliban was hated. I said, like the Taliban, I was exhausting to be around and liked to insinuate myself where I didn't belong.

The other day, an editor at a magazine asked me to think about the State of the Union—as in, the annual address delivered by the president each January. I started to wonder how I was like the United States, and what came to mind is: I'm tired of being hated. I'm tired of being hated when the hatred has been earned by my own selfish acts. I'm tired of being hated for being woman, being Jew, being white feminist.

Hating Trump for four years was like breathing all the time the particles that swirled around us after the Towers went down. Morning, noon, and night we hated. And now, what to do with all the reasons still left to hate?

I'll tell you a story. I find myself in a quandary about a friend about whom I often think, What a fool you are, or, What a danger you are to yourself and others. Still, I like her and look back fondly to times she opened her house to me, hooked me up to people who helped me in travels, promoted my work.

These days, she speaks out openly against COVID vaccines, a position issuing from a haze of metaphysical understandings she has held as long as I've known her. I do not associate with her and will not associate with her. Still, I like her bent toward kindness, and her aesthetic sense, and her personal beauty, and her eagerness to laugh. I like her far more than some people I know whose views I share on how the world works.

Our judgment of the actions of others is a big deal, and we weigh what they've done using moral language. When we alight on a term such as *good* or *progressive*, it quickly unravels as an understanding when we list examples. It's an enchantment of language, I think, not a real thing. Still, to me, some things are right, and some things are wrong. I believe there are facts and not-facts. I have long disapproved of this person. I have long thought to myself while listening to her: don't tell me more, for fear I will have to draw a line.

The other day she emailed to say she'd fallen down a flight of stairs and asked if I would do her a small favor—pick up something she'd bought at a shop— and I said I would. I didn't have a moment's hesitation and didn't think I was inviting the kind of connection we'd had in the past. In truth, she's been unavailable for many years, caught up in a whirlwind of obligations that interest me not at all. Still, I like her.

The reason I'm telling you this story is I like the quandary. The quandary is perhaps the only real subject to write about. Beloved inconsistency. We don't love who we are supposed to love according to an equivalency of *good person, yes, I love you*, and *bad person, I don't love you and be gone*. It's not easy to hate someone you know.

Which brings me to *Ted Lasso*, a show touted as an antidote to hate and that earns a yes from me (along with scads of other people)—this past season it scored twenty Emmy nominations. My first reaction was like that of the English football fans to Ted: *wanker*. Then its methods began to reveal their charms. The fish out of water isn't supposed to be the catalyst for changing his adopted world. In *Northern Exposure*, for example, New Yorker Joel has to learn to become human from the locals in Cicely, Alaska, where he goes to live. But Jason Sudeikis, the star and co-creator of *Lasso* makes Ted funny and lost and weird to such an unusual degree, we go with him.

I read Doreen St. Felix's review of the show in *The New Yorker*. It's called "Ted Lasso Can't Save us." She hates the show, hates that a show centered around a white, fortysomething man from the Midwest—Kansas, to be precise, same as Sudeikis—is such a hit, hates the ironfisted positivity Ted metes out, hates

Jason, too, because she just does. Her right, as Ted would say, not offended.

There is every reason to say puh-lease, not you again, do I have to hear another word from you, male human who is white and has received a lot of opportunity, do I have to hear what you think and what you have to say, I mean, do I really need this, and why should you get more space when you already own the world, more or less? St. Felix thinks *Ted Lasso* is sentimental and is pushing sentimentality as a stance in life to oppose hating things that are repugnant. She doesn't see the show is also about pain *and*. Most of the moments in the show have an *and*. *And* is for more. *And* is water and wind blowing around jasmine petals.

This morning I was thinking about comedy for the hell of it. I was thinking about comedies I like, and I was thinking about the difference between *Ted Lasso* on one hand and, on the other hand, *Veep* and *Succession*, two shows I find funny because they are English-mean as only the English can be mean. Not once in all the years of *Veep* was anyone allowed to be lovable. Even the lovable characters were not lovable because they were too inept and clueless to be lovable. *Succession* is a car accident you have to rubberneck, chronicling a family of Murdock-like billionaires doing vile things to remain billionaires and featuring

two Shakespearean clowns as on-tap scapegoats—
Shiv's husband Tom (Matthew Macfadyen) and the
giant nephew Greg (Nicholas Braun). Their line read-
ings are so straight-faced, idiotically brilliant, I can't
say more right now.

Everyone in *Ted Lasso* is lovable and funny. Not all the
time. But how can lovable be funny at all? I think it
has to do with the characters being aware of who they
are and commenting on the way they are types to some
extent, and also not—shy Nate sitting on a geyser of
ambition, smiling Ted quivering with secret panic
attacks, cocky footballer Jamie smarting from whacks
by his abusive father. Comedy has to be subversive, or
we don't laugh. The subversive aspect of *Ted Lasso* in
season two is the inclusion of an opposite type in the
heart of the show—outsider to the team Sharon the
shrink, a Black woman who is in some kind of pain
and who is not won over by Ted or Tedness, same as
Doreen St. Felix. She's been hired to help Ted discover
what Tedness is, how it evolved as a defense, how it
made him unsexy to his wife, and how he is going to
have to be pleasant *and* or keep suffering.

The show is curious about what makes a man sexy to
women. It gives the male characters permission to
wriggle out of the boxes men get squeezed into that
aren't fun. The fun things, like playing genius football,

get to stay. Everyone knows the shit women get to do together is more fun than what men get to do together. On this show, the men form a group to gossip and think through their relationships and fears without believing it's turning them into pussies. How do you be a man who is sexy to women and doesn't act like a macho prick? Isn't that what we've asked men to think about for the past fifty years? That's what this show is making jokes about.

And now some love for *Promising Young Woman* (2020), which has just become available to stream, written and directed by Emerald Fennell (she directed season two of the feminist thriller *Killing Eve*). The movie excited me. There are lots of things wrong with it. I don't care.

It's about vigilante consciousness-raising! It's about a woman understanding the gang rape that happened to her friend when she was drunk also happened to her, in the sense that no one in the surround of the medical school the women were attending took seriously the charges made against the male students—and still don't, ten or so years later, when the film begins.

Both women drop out of school. The raped one kills herself. The one who survives stages ambushes in bars, pretending to be facedown-drunk in order to shame would-be rapists into the knowledge of what they are. In other entrapping scenarios, she shames the women who collude with the world by saying of the dead woman, "She was drunk. What did she expect?"

I loved the anger of central character Cassie, played with dry wit by Carey Mulligan. I loved her understanding that if there is a single woman on the planet you can get away with raping, or forcing into a child marriage, or maiming for noncompliance with religious and cultural dictates, or for not looking a certain way and dressing a certain way, or having sex a certain way or not having sex a certain way—if there is a single woman on the planet whose body is at the mercy of whatever because it is the body of a woman, then the bodies of all women are at risk for the same treatment.

There is no acting by proxy, no rage by proxy, the movie says. The air, filled with contempt, and the air, filled with the lie that this contempt does not exist, is the only air there is to breathe, and here it drives the female hero mad. It's all she can think about: the air.

Five minutes ago, I was writing about *Ted Lasso* as a palate cleanser to all the hate we've been feeling about Trumpers, antivaxxers, and other kinds of fascists. I was all "give peas a chance," and I was feeling it. And the reason I love aliveness so much is that five minutes later, show me a movie about hate and I'm a dog jumping for a hot dog on a string. I will never be tired of hating, to be honest. It wakes me up, makes me smarter and more logical. How can anyone be female and not be on fire all the time? If they appear cool, it's because they are on fire under their raincoats.

Apartment

The other day I decided to give up my apartment in Manhattan. Manhattan is where I was born and have lived most of my life. If I don't live there again, well, okay.

Becoming a person who does not live in New York City is like waiting for the buzzer to ring before a date, when you dance around to Jimmy Cliff singing, "The Harder They Come." You dance around because you can see the night unfold and you have gotten dressed too early. When I clean out a place, I become lighter. Becoming lighter, I add to the time I have left. Who would not be happy, sitting on the floor of a room you will never see again, tearing a life to shreds?

In 1978, when I moved to my apartment, I was with my dog and Gardner, the artist. My intention was not to die. Other than that, I didn't think far ahead. The rent was $290. I knew a woman who liked me, then turned the opposite, then liked me again. She was moving into the apartment of her boyfriend and said I could have her place. It was on the Upper West Side. I didn't think the Upper West Side was where I should be. In those days, I said okay to all sorts of things I thought were fleeting and that became marriages.

In this type of building, there was a thin rat with a greasy look you had to slip money to in order to get the lease. You would slip one month's rent into his outstretched palm under the table, as the saying goes, and under an actual table, if memory serves. Before moving to this apartment, I had been living in a rental house in East Hampton, where I met Gardner. We rented a truck for the move, and the truck got a flat tire on the Long Island Expressway. It was raining. I was driving the truck. How is this possible? Someone fixed the tire. It was a time in life when these things happened. If it happened now, would I write about it differently?

This morning in the bathtub, I was thinking about sex in the sense of "why not follow an impulse." The nature of sex is something independent of language. With language, we conjure things that are not here and not now, things postponed and imagined. Language creates images in the mind. Why would you need images in the mind? In one theory of the origin of language, our primate ancestors needed to cooperate with members of different troupes to fend off larger predators while they hacked off meat from a dead carcass in the woods down the road. They would need to imagine food not here and not now to band together, and they would need combinations of sounds and gestures they all understood that signified "dead animal" and "down the road."

Sex, on the other hand, is right here and right now. Sex is like Blue Jay A tricking Blue Jay B into dropping that pumpkin seed so Blue Jay A can snap it up and fly away.

In the bathtub, I was thinking about a man I took one look at years ago and knew I was finished. He wasn't the kind of man used to arousing this reaction, and I think when he saw he had become an object of such obvious desire it was comic and poignant and he couldn't turn away. I could be wrong.

I smile when people think I know what I want. I'm not the kind who can picture the dead animal down the road that would make a nice filling for a sandwich if only you could walk over and hack off the meat. I took the apartment for sex. The city was sex. I thought if you felt an impulse and you were a female human, you should do what a man would do, which is what a dog would do without foreseeing the consequences. I thought I should learn all I could learn about sex for no reason other than I was curious. And there was nothing to stop me. I lived in the apartment alone all those years. Solitude is sex. People would stay over, but they didn't live there.

Years ago, maybe eight or nine, I packed up the apartment in order to sublet it to a friend and move my belongings to Arizona, where the man I live with now was teaching at a university. With a New York City rent-stabilized apartment, you have to be in residence for six months and one day of every year or risk losing it, unless you install a tenant the landlord approves of, and then only for two years maximum. We packed the books into towers of boxes. We had a sale, during which I watched my beloved bike wheeled away and other items I had depended on drift off.

I did not want to disappoint the man I live with now, but I could feel myself moving along on a conveyer belt, much like the conveyor belt I had stepped onto when, at nineteen, I agreed to marry a lovely young man in order to secure another apartment—this one Downtown—that required my father to cosign the lease. My father said he would sign the lease if I agreed to marry the young man I was living with.

I did not want to get married, and I did not want to

move my belongings to Arizona. I did not want to spend even one hour in Arizona during the years I was there in order to be with the man I live with now. I did not think my belongings should move west when, in time, I hoped we would together move east.

The man I live with now could see I was sad. After a few days of packing and negotiating with the landlord, he said, "Don't do it. Keep the apartment. Spend the time you need to here. We'll be okay." And that's what we did. And that is one of the reasons I have wanted to build a life with this person—that, and I like talking to him.

In the years I shuttled between New York and Arizona, I did not tire of solitude. In all the years I spent in Arizona, I never wanted to part from the man I live with now.

He believes there are two-way doors and one-way doors. With two-way doors, you go in one direction and go back in the other direction. With one-way doors, you can't go back. The example he gives is, "No culture that gave up hunting and gathering for agriculture ever went back to hunting and gathering. Once you've got pottery, you can't imagine a life without it." If I give up the apartment, he believes I cannot live in New York City again. I believe there is only one

one-way door, and that is death. Being done with this place is like starting an affair. I already miss New York.

In the apartment the other day, the art gone, the rugs gone, some of the smaller furniture gone, it's already no longer where I ever lived. It looks like the set for a play that is yet to be built, props strewn about for scenes that are disappearing as objects are packed into boxes. The way I live in the past is to make the same mistakes I have always made.

The apartment looks like an archaeological site without a history of importance, not because nothing happened there but because whatever happened there happened to someone who cared. Time feels sped up, as if there is all the time in the world to do nothing important. It was always just living I was doing.

Leaves are falling onto the plants in the garden, and it's impossible to keep the beds neat. Still, I pick out the leaves and sweep in front of the beds. Two deer are feeding on a lawn nearby. Yesterday, the man I live with now pulled a small tick off my back. I took two doses of doxycycline in case the tick had transmitted a disease. In the apartment the other day, I threw clothes I wore in the '80s, '90s, and so on into plastic bags. Some of the clothes still fit. But that's no longer enough.

New Place

Today in the apartment we found four large envelopes marked LETTERS. Richard said, "There's probably a book in there." Like making a quilt from all the clothes you've ever worn, cut into tiny squares.

I want the house to eat my other lives. You only need one skin at a time. Mostly, the letters we write are letters of love, and that's why I have saved them, maybe, to prove I was loved.

I read "My Gentile Region" by Gary Shteyngart in last week's *New Yorker*, about a botched circumcision performed when he was seven and had emigrated to the United States from Soviet Russia. Attempts to correct the surgery in later life fail, stirring a contemplation of fragile male parts rarely made public. Shteyngart writes with customary wit and candor, sadness and beauty, detailing pain that cannot be resolved. There is careful observation of the penis here—not so much of women. Early on, he writes, "I have always imagined that beyond its pleasurable utility the penis must be an incomprehensible thing to most heterosexual women, like a walrus wearing a cape that shows up every once in a while to perform a quick round of gardening."

Gary! To heterosexual women—and I think I can speak for all of them—the penis is not any kind of marine mammal. The penis is a confidant you can speak to for hours, a hand puppet, a sculptural ornament you can shift around—especially in the morning, with its bump of hello before it wanders off to make tea. It is beautiful and tasty, more than a dildo made of flesh, and I mean really a friend I wouldn't know what to do without, although I have done without it for considerable periods, and when, after a long absence, it has again poked out from a pair of trousers, I have felt a peace wash over me.

I'm going through a catalog of books Norton is publishing, and I come across *The Authority Gap: Why Women Are Still Taken Less Seriously Than Men—and What We Can Do About It* by Mary Ann Sieghart. I try to remember a time when I took seriously the authority of men, and I can see it over there, wrapped in gray fog. The education I would require to become a human being was delivered by women. Individual men were smart and lovable and had things to tell me I enjoyed hearing about. But for me, everything depended on the authority of women because the authority of men was going to destroy my chance to know anything I would come to care about.

There's a woman at West Elm, I adore her. It's time to swap out the ceiling fixtures that came with the house. The granite table that will be moving here in a month weighs maybe eight hundred pounds. The woman I love at West Elm acts like she cares, to the extent we all know nothing we are talking about matters.

Before West Elm, the man I live with went to the hospital in Albany to see his endocrinologist and learned he had killed his A1C, a number that means you are maintaining your blood sugars in the kind of range you can expect to enjoy for some time a granite table and above it a light fixture made of LED rods that burn for a finite number of years. "The lights," I said to the woman I love, "will still be burning when we are long dead." She laughed.

After West Elm, we visited the company that supplied fixtures for our bathroom. A man we met who does electricals also does plumbing—he's a genius—and was about to swap out cartridges for our fancy German faucets that leak when he noticed both cartridges were marked LEFT. It was like getting sent two left shoes.

It turned out the boxes were marked LEFT, but the cartridges were both for right faucets. A nice woman was alone in the store. There were Halloween candies in a bowl, including small packets of M&M's I shoved in my pocket. Richard ate one. His sugar was dropping. His pump was shrieking. I said to the nice woman, "Do you think we will have to go to Germany to get a right cartridge and a left cartridge?" She said, "Probably not."

The number of cartoons in *The New Yorker* I have ever found amusing is zero. In the latest episode of *The Morning Show*, when Holland Taylor says with pride that she is a cockroach and will still be standing when everyone else at the TV network is a shriveled husk, I was reminded of the giant water bugs I could never banish from my apartment on Charles Street, and I could still hear their carapaces scraping the wide plank floors as they scuttled from the living room to the kitchen. When you are awake in the middle of the night, time stretches out in both directions, pulled thin at the edges without breaking, like pizza dough, and that's the thrill of solitude. In photographs of Samuel Beckett, no matter what he's wearing, his *chic* is to look like the chic is accidental.

The house smells of bananas. A cloud of fruit flies hovers over the bananas in a bowl. There's nothing for it but to bake the bananas, same as leaving the apartment. I could pick up the phone and hear the voice of anyone from the past and say, "What is going on in your life? It's nice of you to think of me."

Actually, I would do no such thing. Something of what I have just written has a tinge of truth. Today I felt a ripple of unease flowing through me, like an underground stream you can't easily locate. I wonder if I will ever again walk the streets of New York with good posture. It was a different kind of happiness I was thinking about—I'm separate and awake in the night. It was happiness blushed with anxiety and the possibility of appearing foolish. Because I looked better, I could bear it.

I am hate-watching *Scenes from a Marriage* by Israeli writer/director Hagai Levi. Episode four brought back memories of the time we all slept with orthodox Jewish men, and as soon as the sex was over, the men got up and washed off their dicks because pussy juice is unclean. We thought it was so sexy! It brought back memories of the time we slept with men and thought the sex was good, and afterward they got dressed and said they were planning to have a baby with someone else. Like you couldn't have mentioned that before the sex? We thought that was so macho, and we pined ever after for the guy. It brought back memories of fucking doggy style, so the dick was ramming against your cervix and it really hurt and there was no clitoral contact and it was impossible to come unless you were so hot for any kind of sex in any position you could think yourself off. This was supposed to be the hottest of hot sex positions—it said so in all the movies and all the TV shows—and we knew it was the worst, but hey, who were we to argue? It brought back memories of the time the guy was a dick in all these ways and was still the hero of the story for taking care of his own child (!) and the one who was done to in the mind of the writers and directors, because the guy was them. And who were we to disagree?

I wrote this on Facebook and had to explain to more than one reader I was being sarcastic and conjuring a collective female experience I was making up. I have never had sex with an orthodox Jewish man who washed off his dick like the character does on the show. I had to say this, and also why don't you stab me through the heart for making me explain comedy.

Today

I told the landlord I'm not signing a new lease. Soon, never again the hallways with their chipped tiles and the great vaulting ugly of the lobby. The landlord had been measuring me for a coffin for years and was perhaps relieved she wouldn't have to spring for one. I felt so free when I got off the phone, all I could do was dance around.

I packed plates designed by Andrée Putman I had saved for the future. There's no time like the future. I still have the collar and tags of my dog I used to keep on the front door. I will pack them and the copper urn that looks like a canister of radioactive waste and contains my father's ashes.

Every place you leave is a crime scene. The receipts in drawers, the tubes in the medicine cabinet are evidence. What is the crime? I come as the cleaner, the fixer, the one with the bucket and gloves. I work fast, in order to make a clean getaway.

Little by little, the apartment—with the abstract paintings Gardner made and sculptural furniture he designed—is being installed in the living room, like one of those period rooms in a museum. I have not yet packed pictures of me with my dog and other people I knew that line the walls of the kitchen. Where will they go in the life I am living now? It doesn't matter.

Each day, the days before matter less. I don't think anyone is going back to how things were. I am beginning to doubt there is such a thing as a happy memory because memory itself is not a happy state of mind. Happiness is a dog running in fall air, tongue out, eyes shining. How marvelous to live long enough to escape your past.

It's warm for a few more nights. I want these days to stretch to the farthest reaches of my imagination. I'm digging up annuals from the beds. They don't want to come inside. It was the windows and walls I liked about the house. Next week is my birthday. I can't get over how much less I care about things I've done wrong. Please come and cut the back of my hair.

A moment ago, this sentence formed: It's important in life not to be well-thought-of. I mean to become so dependent on being well-thought-of, you don't do the things and think the thoughts that make a person not well-thought-of.

On the street a little while ago, a woman from the building says she is sorry I'm leaving. I tell her I'm not sorry. Then, as she moves toward the corner with her little white dog, I understand she is saying she is sorry she's not leaving.

You come to the airport with a ticket to A. There's a blizzard, and your flight is canceled. One by one, other flights are canceled. You are dying to arrive at your destination, and suddenly one flight is announced. It will land at an airport a distance from the place you want to get to. You don't know how you will get from point B, where you will land, to point A, where you want to go. You get on the plane to point B. You get on the plane that is leaving the airport. Happiest story of my life.

Acknowledgments

Fifteen years ago, I started visiting Arizona, where Richard Toon was teaching, and I couldn't find a place to situate myself that felt like a party I wanted to be at. In 2009, I joined Facebook. It was already old news, I was told, but you could write without counting the characters. I didn't know the protocols of social media. I was lonely and wanted to write as if I were talking to someone. I posted little pieces of fiction. Little pieces of memoir. Reactions to things that were happening in the world. I wrote about movies and TV shows I was watching, books I was reading, experiences in the desert and other places I was moving through. Without meaning to, I was practicing a form of hybrid writing that jumps around these genres and smushes them together the way they are smushed together in this book, which is a long way of saying thank you, friends on Facebook. All of you! Many chunks of this book were prompted by your posts. Thanks for being smart, informed, funny, caring, questioning. Did I mention funny?

Thanks to Steve Mitchell, editor of Scuppernong Editions, who read my posts on Facebook and thought they could be the basis of a book and in 2019 published *Everything is Personal, Notes on Now*.

Thanks beyond thanks to editors Jennifer Baumgardner, Dale Peck, John Oakes, Marco Roth, Mark Krotov, and Jeffery Renard Allen for publishing some of the pieces that appear here and supporting the voice of intimacy that ties things together. Ish.

Thanks to Dottir Press and especially to Jennifer Baumgardner, Larissa Melo Pienkowski, Kait Heacock, Noelle McManus, and Drew Stevens. Thanks Andrew Saulter for the cover.

Thanks to the friends I adore because they are adorable and because they read my stuff before I send it off: Gordon Beeferman, Navtej Dhillon, Wendy Sibbison, Emily Upham, and Mike Levine.

Thanks to Richard Toon for being my buddy in all things and for co-inventing the writing practice we share most nights before, these days in Pandemica, drinking cocktails and streaming something. Before there are posts on Facebook, there are pieces sketched in a notebook, sitting in a room somewhere across from Richard, who is writing in his notebook, and when we finish and look up, I always say, "You read first." Because I can't wait to hear what he will say.